PIOUS PROPERTY

PIOUS PROPERTY

ISLAMIC MORTGAGES IN THE UNITED STATES

BILL MAURER

RUSSELL SAGE FOUNDATION • NEW YORK

The Russell Sage Foundation

The Russell Sage Foundation, one of the oldest of America's general purpose foundations, was established in 1907 by Mrs. Margaret Olivia Sage for "the improvement of social and living conditions in the United States." The Foundation seeks to fulfill this mandate by fostering the development and dissemination of knowledge about the country's political, social, and economic problems. While the Foundation endeavors to assure the accuracy and objectivity of each book it publishes, the conclusions and interpretations in Russell Sage Foundation publications are those of the authors and not of the Foundation, its Trustees, or its staff. Publication by Russell Sage, therefore, does not imply Foundation endorsement.

Library of Congress Cataloging-in-Publication Data

Maurer, Bill, 1968–
  Pious property : Islamic mortgages in the United States / Bill Maurer.
    p.   cm.
  Includes bibliographical references and index.
  ISBN 0-87154-581-0
    1. Mortgage loans—United States.   2. Finance (Islamic law)   3. Muslims—United States.   I. Title.

HG2040.5.U5M38 2006
332.7′22′0882970973—dc22   2005044411

The paper used in this publication meets the minimum requirements of American National Standard for Information Sciences—Permanence of Paper for Printed Library Materials. ANSI Z39.48-1992.

Text design by Genna Patacsil.

RUSSELL SAGE FOUNDATION
112 East 64th Street, New York, New York 10021
10   9   8   7   6   5   4   3   2   1

CONTENTS

About the Author   vii

Acknowledgments   ix

Glossary of Arabic Terms   xiii

Introduction   1

Chapter 1   What Is a Mortgage?
             The History of a Religious Concept   14

Chapter 2   What Is an Islamic Mortgage?   28

Chapter 3   Postmodern and Puritan:
             A Tale of Two Companies   44

Chapter 4   Who Wants Islamic Mortgage Alternatives?   56

Chapter 5   Choosing an Islamic Mortgage Alternative   74

Chapter 6   The Securitization of Islamic Mortgages   85

Chapter 7   Home Financing and the Transformation
             of American Islamic Law   93

Chapter 8   Conclusion   98

             Notes   103

             References   109

             Index   117

ABOUT THE AUTHOR

BILL MAURER is associate professor of anthropology at the University of California, Irvine.

ACKNOWLEDGMENTS

This short book was a labor of love—love for an subject that would not let me go while I was in the middle of a larger research project on Islamic banking, alternative currencies, and the problem of money in social analysis. That subject is the Islamic mortgage contract, which captivated my imagination from the moment I was first introduced to it. Perhaps it was because I had recently taken out a mortgage for my own first house. Perhaps it was because Islamic mortgages opened my eyes to the array of contractual forms that structure and animate Islamic banking and helped me map out each kind of contract as a hypothetical way to finance real estate. There is something about the tangibility of real estate as an application of finance and property law that makes it easier to understand the complexities of those laws. Finance, after all, is highly abstract and complicated. Real estate, land, is solid material; it is the ground we walk on, the buildings we live in.

At the same time, the Islamic mortgage dazzled me. The anthropologist Marilyn Strathern (1999, 10, 11) writes that during fieldwork one is always expecting to be surprised. The record of fieldwork—the ethnographic text—attempts to recapture that sense of expectation. "An initial surprise becomes a suspension, a dazzle, and some kinds of 'special knowledge' are more likely to dazzle than others. One is held," Strathern writes, "on the threshold of understanding." I continued to be held on that threshold of understanding throughout my relationship with the Islamic mortgage. This book is a record of our relationship.

It is also a record of the other important relationships that facilitated the project on which it is based. Research was supported by two grants from the Russell Sage Foundation, and I would like to express my deep thanks to Stephanie Platz, formerly at Russell Sage, for her intellectual encouragement and collegiality throughout the project, as well as a careful and critical reading of the entire manuscript. I would also like to thank Stephanie, the Russell Sage Foundation, and the Social Science Research Council for providing venues at which I was able to discuss this project with other scholars working on Islam in the United States in the aftermath of September 11, 2001.

Several colleagues have been indispensable. Karen Leonard continues to encourage my work by constantly bringing new sources and new ideas to my attention. I have benefited from conversations with Charles Hirschkind, Kathleen Moore, Saba Mahmood, Hirokazu Miyazaki, Nadine Naber, Annelise Riles, Gregory Starrett, and Kaushik Sunder Rajan. Anita Iannucci, Robert Newcomb, and Harold Dyck at the Center for Statistical Consulting at the University of California at Irvine provided some statistical guidance. I would also like to thank Mike Burton for discussions about the models in chapter 4. I thank Tom Boellstorff and Karen Hunt Ahmed for reading and providing comments on the entire manuscript. Thanks to Tom too for helping create the figures in chapter 3. I also owe a huge debt of thanks to Tasneem Siddiqui, who served as a research assistant for this project and conducted some of the interviews discussed in this book. Tasneem also read and commented on the entire manuscript, and I thank her for her good humor and critical eye. I would also like to thank Suzanne Nichols and two anonymous reviewers for useful critical commentary on the manuscript. I thank Genna Patacsil and Cindy Buck for their assistance with the copyediting and production of this volume.

The project could not have been attempted, of course, without the generous participation of all those who agreed to be interviewed and who helped me muddle through the field of home financing, Islamic or otherwise. It goes without saying that all errors or inconsistencies in what follows are my responsibility alone and that the opinions presented here do not reflect those of any funding agency, company, or other agent besides myself.

Little of the material presented here will be surprising to those in the field of Islamic home finance. Following the conventions of anthropological writing and ethics protocols, I have made interviewees and conversation partners anonymous and disguised the identities of two companies whose applicant pools I examine in some detail in chapters 3, 4, and 5. I also disguise these companies' identities whenever they come up in interviews or conversations. I know in advance that the effort to disguise some identities will probably fail for readers familiar with the field, but I feel that it is important to adhere to the form of the ethical practice. To do otherwise might give the impression that my own efforts are ultimately about adjudicating between these two companies' different mortgage models, and such adjudication is not my concern or intention. Furthermore, this book should not be taken as a guide to choosing an Islamic mortgage replacement product. Interested readers should consult trusted advisers, friends, and the wealth of material being produced by those marketing such products as well as those critical of them. This book is dedicated to Gina Wallar, Brian Ulaszewski, and David Hernandez, who continually create for me new understandings of the relationship between property, civic virtue, community, and family.

GLOSSARY OF ARABIC TERMS[1]

faqih jurist
fard obligation
fatwa jurisprudential ruling
fiqh jurisprudence
fiqh-ul-hiyal jurisprudence of legal stratagems
fiqh-ul-mu'amalat jurisprudence of financial transactions
halal Islamically acceptable
haram Islamically forbidden
ijara a leasing contract
ijtihad scriptural interpretation
istisna a contract under which a manufacturer or contractor agrees to build something at a future date
mudaraba a profit-and-loss-sharing contract
murabaha a contract for the sale of an existing item at a markup (cost-plus)
musharaka a corporate partnership
qiyas reasoning by analogy
riba unfair or illegitimate increase; usury or interest
riba al-fadl riba by excess
riba al-nasi'a increase through deferment
sadaqa voluntary alms
shari'a Islamic law
sukuk the plural form of the Arabic word for deed or legal document; used to refer to Islamically permissible securities
taqlid imitation
umma world community of Muslims
zakat religiously mandated alms

INTRODUCTION

I slamic banking and finance is a growth sector in the world economy. It seeks to create and market financial instruments and investment vehicles that adhere to Islam's prohibition of interest. There are various estimates of its size and significance. According to one, Islamic finance has grown from around $50 million to over $250 billion and spread to seventy-five countries in only ten years (Janahi 2004). The Dow Jones Islamic Market Index, created in 1999, lists over 1,900 stocks with a market capitalization of over $11 trillion that have been screened to ensure compliance with Islamic law.[1] Many of the largest multinational banks now have "Islamic windows" that offer financial services and products in compliance with Islamic law. Measured in terms of transactions, Citibank is the largest bank offering such "Islamic" services, having managed $6 billion in "shari'a-compliant" funds since 1996 (Pope 2005). The U.S. Department of Treasury appointed its first Islamic banking "scholar-in-residence" in June 2004. Meanwhile, Muslims the world over hold around $180 billion in bank funds. This represents an untapped market to industry analysts, who expect up to 15 percent growth over the first decade of the twenty-first century (Day and Jayasankaran 2003).

Despite the growth and potential of Islamic banking and finance, however, many commentators and critics question the whole endeavor. In a recent book, the economist Timur Kuran (2004) criticizes Islamic banking as an ideological smoke screen disguising anti-Western interests and promoting inefficient economic thinking. It may serve to bolster the Islamic credentials of the elites who support it, but it does little to address the pressing economic needs of Muslims worldwide. Abdullah Saeed (1998, 1999), in documenting the history of Islamic banking, notes the serious tensions between those who seek to create a new economic or social utopia and those who seek to create a profit-generating brand name

1

to tap into an emerging market niche. Many commentators, like Frank Vogel and Samuel Hayes (1998), take a more pragmatic point of view: no matter how it is evaluated, and whatever the intentions of its promoters, Islamic banking exists, and it is attracting intellectual and economic attention. In another work (Maurer 2005), I argue that Islamic banking restages some of the animating problematics of contemporary social theory as well as those of economic exchange more broadly. In doing so, I argue, it also reveals elements of conventional (that is, non-Islamic) finance and helps us better to see the intertwining of social domains we tend to keep separate analytically, such as religion and economics, or moral values and economic value (Stark 2002).

My concern in this book is much smaller in scale, and closer to home. In the course of my research on Islamic banking I became fascinated with experiments going on in the United States and elsewhere to provide Islamically acceptable financing for purchasing a home. When I first began research on Islamic banking in 1998, there was only one Islamic mortgage provider in the United States of any significance, although there had been several earlier failed attempts. As of June 2005, there were at least seven, two of which came into being as I was completing this book. All of the growth has taken place since 2002. The number of applications for Islamic mortgages nationally increased sixfold, from 344 to 2,163, between 2002 and 2003.[2] Although the growth has been dramatic, the absolute numbers are small. Are Islamic mortgages just a blip on the radar screen of American home finance or global Islamic banking? Or do they mark something more significant? My answer obviously leans toward the latter conclusion, though this answer is not as direct as one might at first suppose. The argument of this book is that Islamic mortgages in the United States provide a window into an ongoing transformation in Muslim Americans' understanding of Islamic law and that this transformation has been spurred as much by American government and bureaucracy as by shari'a scholarship or traditional religious interpretation.

Mortgage lending in the West historically has had a troubled relationship to usury. The common law settled the issue in the 1600s. In Islam, however, the debate over usury has had a different history, one closely related to the question of interpretation (ijtihad) and the finality of Islamic law (shari'a) and jurisprudence (fiqh). Ijtihad opened doors for Islamic financial experimentation in the twentieth century, and Islamic mortgages represent one genre of experimentation. Islamic mortgages are a shari'a-compliant financial product that is within the reach and, importantly, the conceptual universe of most people in the United States.

While complicated mutual fund portfolios and Islamic futures or hedge funds remain outside the intellectual and economic ken of many Americans, a mortgage is integral to the American dream of homeownership and was promoted throughout the twentieth century as part and parcel of democratic equality and opportunity. Several factors have come together since 2000 to spur the growth of Islamic mortgages: the regulatory rulings of certain government agencies, most notably the Office of the Comptroller of the Currency (OCC); the financial support of Freddie Mac and Fannie Mae, the government agencies that historically have provided liquidity to mortgage markets and been committed to extending home financing to underserved populations; a renewed sense of Islamic identity in the wake of the terrorist attacks of September 11, 2001; and the conjuncture of the post-9/11 stock market decline with the continuation of historically low interest rates, which has made homeownership a more attractive investment than stocks. Interestingly, these factors have combined to spur the development of several different models for an Islamic mortgage.

This book considers two of the most important. At first glance, and to an outsider, one product seems more shari'a-compliant than the other—that is, it more closely seems to adhere to the prohibition of interest—but in fact more conservative Muslims gravitate toward the other product. I should stress at the outset my own ambivalence in declaring one product more or less compliant than the other and in deciding on the characteristics that identify a person as more or less conservative. (A side argument of this book is that such evaluations do not adequately capture the nuances of Islamic law or the shifting terrain of Muslim identity in the United States. Non-Muslim Americans' stereotypes of Muslims do not square neatly with the reality; moreover, the traditional views shared by many Americans of what constitutes political, social, economic, and religious conservatism or liberalism are often equally at odds with Muslim identity.) Muslim Americans choose their mortgage product less because of its formal qualities than because of its endorsement by prominent scholars. The opinions of these scholars connect up with the government's bureaucratic rulings and techniques developed by state regulatory agencies and government-sponsored enterprises like Fannie Mae. In other words, Islamic mortgages are a hybrid creation of certain shari'a scholars, the financial sector, and the U.S. government. What begins as a story about finance thus becomes a story about the role of scholarly authority and bureaucratic expertise in the shaping of Islamic law and Muslim identity in the United States.

THE SCOPE OF THE BOOK

This book is based on fieldwork conducted between 2002 and 2004 in southern California among Muslim Americans interested in Islamic mortgages and professionals involved in creating and marketing Islamic mortgage products. That fieldwork involved face-to-face, email, and telephone interviews, as well as informal conversations. My research also made use of a collection of archival material related to the development of Islamic home financing, including stories in the mass media, legal documents, religious and regulatory rulings, and the proclamations of prominent individuals in the field. I attempt here not only to provide a history of the development of Islamic home financing but also to convey a sense of the wider conversation about Islamic mortgages that is taking place in the United States today. The book sets a baseline against which future data on this emerging field can be compared.

The book does not review the development of Islamic mortgages in other countries that have recently witnessed the development of new methods of home financing, such as Malaysia and the United Kingdom. As I was completing this book, in fact, a controversy erupted in the United Kingdom over the legitimacy of the HSBC bank's lease-to-purchase mortgage replacement product. I discuss this controversy briefly in chapter 2, but I did not conduct extensive research outside the United States for this project, and as I make clear in the conclusion (chapter 8), I think something unique is going on in the world of *American* Islamic mortgages that is not likely to be replicated elsewhere, at least for now, because of the role of government-sponsored enterprises like Freddie Mac and Fannie Mae. In providing liquidity and creating a secondary market for mortgage financing in this country, these enterprises are deeply connected to the American preoccupation with property ownership as the cornerstone of citizenship.

I use several terms to refer to the object of my study. They all should be taken to refer to the same set of contractual forms and relationships described in what follows. For simplicity's sake, I prefer the term "Islamic mortgage," though, as we will see, technically the Islamic mortgage is not a mortgage at all—or rather, it is *usually* not a mortgage. It is also not singular but takes several contractual forms. I explain those different forms in detail in this volume, but I use the term "Islamic mortgage" to refer to the whole set. Companies offering them tend to use terms like "Islamic mortgage alternative" or "Islamic mortgage replacement product." I also employ these terms interchangeably with "Islamic mortgage."

This book also speaks to several literatures in anthropology and the social sciences more broadly. Most directly, it is inspired by recent work across the social sciences on the social and cultural constitution of finance and financial markets (for example, Abolafia 1996; Helleiner 1994; Hertz 1998; Knorr Cetina and Bruegger 2000; MacKenzie 2003; Pryke and Allen 2000; Thrift 2000; Tickell 2000; Tsing 2000; Zaloom 2003). This work often begins from Michel Callon's (1998) insight that "the economy" is not an autonomous domain. It is not simply "embedded" in larger social fields (Granovetter 1985) but rather is actively created and performed by systems of expert knowledge like the academic discipline of economics. Economics, Callon argues, formats the economy, structures it, and then purports to explain in neutral, objective terms what it itself has created. Economies are "embedded" in economic theories as much as they are in wider social contexts. This approach to finance and economics requires attention to the form of those expert knowledges as much as to their content (see Maurer 2005; Miyazaki 2003; Riles 2004). Islamic banking and finance, as an effort consciously and critically to re-create some of the forms and formats of financial activity by writing new kinds of contracts and developing new products and transactions, is a signal case of what Callon terms the "performation" of the economy.

To date, however, most of the literature on the sociology and anthropology of finance has been concerned with large-scale processes and the financial professionals involved in big trades and international markets. The literature has focused on "the trading of financial instruments not designed for consumption" and on those aspects of the markets where "the 'goods' are contracts . . . that circulate rather than being channeled to end consumers" (Knorr Cetina and Preda 2005, 4). This book, in contrast, focuses precisely on contracts channeled to consumers; moreover, most consumers in this target market are people of relatively modest means compared to those who routinely deal in transactions like futures and options. The emphasis is on the retail consumer, though the creation of an equity market in Islamic mortgage paper does become an important part of the story, especially when we look more closely into the role of Freddie Mac and Fannie Mae and the creation of Islamically permissible, mortgage-backed securities. This book also attends to the role of regulators, the state, government-sponsored enterprises, and communities of scholarship in the construction of a financial market.

I seek here to contribute in a small way to the emerging literature on Muslims in the United States (see Haddad and Esposito 1998; Leonard 2003). In the aftermath of September 11, 2001, both media and scholarly accounts of Islam have focused on a relatively well defined but poorly theorized set of issues that have to do with the apparent irreconcilability of Islam with Western democratic ideals. A lot of ink has been spilled over the head-scarf debate; the relationship between Islam and human rights and democracy (with scant attention to the often awkward relationship between other religious traditions and human rights and democracy); and whether Islam is inherently illiberal (again, that the same question could be asked with regard to other monotheisms has received scant attention). This book tries to shift the discussion to topics we do not usually associate with Islam and Muslims and, in doing so, to jostle some stereotypes.

There has been some scholarship on Islamic law in the United States (see Leonard 2003, 86–92), and the role of new spokespeople with little training in fiqh (jurisprudence) in setting the agenda (Abou El Fadl 1998) has been debated. There has also been work on the efforts of Muslims to navigate the American legal terrain (Moore 1995). This book contributes to the analysis of legal scholarly authority among American Muslims. The emerging patterns of authority discussed in this volume are exclusively concerned with finance, however, and thus much work remains to be done on the subject with respect to other areas of everyday life; great debate revolves, for instance, around marriage, sex, and the family.

Homeownership has been a central component of middle-class American identity since the end of World War II, and the idea that citizenship and property go hand in hand has both a romantic (Thomas Paine, Thomas Jefferson) and a sordid (slavery, poll taxes, disenfranchisement, dispossession of Native Americans) history in this country. To the extent that Islamic mortgages afford Muslim Americans who seek to avoid interest a means of owning "a piece of the rock," as one Islamic finance professional put it to me, Islamic mortgages contribute to the economic and cultural citizenship of Muslim Americans, as well as perhaps to their "Americanization." At the same time, I am skeptical of approaches to Muslim American identity that implicitly or explicitly embrace an "acculturation" rubric. As I demonstrate in what follows, it is sometimes difficult to determine the direction of the acculturation—from "Muslim" to "American," or vice versa. Both America and Islam, after all, have pretensions to universality and acultural transcendence. Even before the presidency of George W. Bush, many Americans have viewed America's model of freedom, democracy, and property to be a historical inevitability that can and should be extended to everyone in the world (according to many in power, by force, if necessary). Islam understands itself as the perfection of monotheism and a universal and total way of life that transcends cultural particularity. What happens in the interface of two such universalisms?

This book uses a variety of methods to describe Islamic mortgages. I have tried to write in an accessible style and to avoid extensive literature reviews, theoretical debates, and the specialized languages of my fields. Yet I also hope to demonstrate the usefulness of anthropological ethnography for social analysis. Ethnography has become, curiously, both increasingly marginalized and increasingly popular in fields that have tended to be dominated by formal modeling or quantitative analysis. When ethnography is taken up in those fields or parsed as "qualitative methodology," it is often reduced to formal interviewing and content analysis. When quantitative methods are used in interviewing, the researcher often turns the interviewee into a case subject and attempts to make generalizable claims about the kinds of things people with x or y characteristics say or believe. Similarly, in content analysis meaningful themes in textual data are often decontextualized and turned into variables that can then be entered into a regression analysis.

This is fine for what it can accomplish, and the reader will see that one chapter of this book relies entirely on quantitative methods. But such quantitative methods are not anthropological ethnography. One sets out in anthropological ethnography never knowing in advance what one might find, prepared only to be surprised or even bedazzled. Many anthropologists, myself among them, still maintain a theoretical and ethical commitment to the ethnographic methodology of one of our field's founding figures, Bronislaw Malinowski, whose standards for "participant-observation" demanded that the researcher observe, participate in, and record *all* features of the social and cultural life of the population under study. We may feel daunted by the task, and the unfettered empiricist orientation to knowledge formation of ethnographic methodology may make us queasy (see Maurer 2005). But we still think that it can generate a kind of knowledge that other methods cannot. Returning to our field notes or digging in our memories, we continually come upon small things we may have brushed aside at the time that now speak volumes to our current predicaments, be they intellectual, political, or ethical.

Anthropology, Marilyn Strathern (2004, 5–6) contends, is

> the deliberate attempt to generate more data than the investigator is aware of at the time of collection. . . . Rather than devising research protocols that will purify the data in advance of analysis, the anthro-

pologist embarks on a participatory exercise which yields materials
for which analytical protocols are often devised after the fact. In the
field, the ethnographer may work from indirection, creating tangents from which the principal subject can be observed. . . . But what
is tangent at one stage may become central at the next.

And sometimes following tangents is the only route to any real knowledge about a thing.

THE AMERICAN MUSLIM FINANCIAL MARKET

How many Muslims live in the United States? Knowing the answer to
that question would provide a sense of the size of the potential market for
Islamic financial services and thus a way to gauge its significance. But
this is a question of great controversy. The U.S. census does not collect
information on religious affiliation. The 2001 American Religious Identification Survey, based on a random telephone survey and an open-ended
question that generated respondents' self-descriptions, reported 1.1 million Muslims (U.S. Department of Commerce 2005). A study commis-
sioned by the American Jewish Committee put the estimate between 1.4
million and 2.8 million (Watanabe 2001). American Muslim organizations and one demographic analysis put the figure closer to 7 million
(Watanabe 2001; see also Leonard 2003, 4). At the low end, then, Muslims represent 0.5 percent of the overall U.S. population, and 3 percent at
the high end.

How significant would it be for the potential Islamic mortgage market
if the high estimate were correct? By way of comparison, consider the
Muslim population of the United Kingdom. The U.K. census, which does
collect information on religious identification, reported a population of
1.6 million Muslims, or 2.7 percent of the population, in 2001. This figure corresponds roughly to British Muslim organizations' own estimates
of their numbers, according to the Muslim Council of Britain. But it is not
just population statistics that tell the story here. Business Insights, a
strategic market analysis and research firm, published a special report on
the U.K. mortgage market outlook in 2004 in which Islamic mortgages
were identified as an important emerging niche sector (Kubis-Labiak
2004). In 2003 two large multinational banks, United National Bank and
HSBC, joined the Ahli United Bank (formerly United Bank of Kuwait) in
offering Islamic mortgage products in the United Kingdom, and the
British Treasury abolished the double-charging of the stamp tax on Is-

lamic mortgages (see Bank of England 2003, 240).[3] It is clear then that, in Britain, 3 percent would be considered enough to launch major new product and marketing initiatives and to change tax policy. Muslims there are definitely seen as an untapped market.

It is less clear whether finance professionals in the United States view Muslims as a potential market. Part of the difficulty has to do with the slotting of Muslims in the United States into the "immigrant" category, often despite their place of birth or country of citizenship. This perception of all Muslims as immigrants has been especially pervasive since September 11, 2001, but it affected policy toward Muslims even before then. If Muslims are "immigrants," then the first question many ask is whether they are bringing attitudes or experiences with Islamic financial services and products with them from their countries of origin. While there has been no systematic research on Muslims' attitudes toward mortgage financing across different countries, there has been some work on determinants of the consumption of other kinds of financial services and instruments, such as life insurance. In these other financial areas the evidence is ambiguous at best. Having a large Muslim population does seem to correlate with a low level of life insurance consumption across different countries. But personal income, inflation, and other factors like the institutional development of the banking sector are also strong predictors. Since most of the world's Muslims live in countries that lack strongly developed banking institutions, it is difficult to say whether religion or underdevelopment plays a greater role in life insurance consumption (Beck and Webb 2003). Furthermore, immigrants' prior experiences with financial institutions of any type are affected by their economic and social class, regardless of their religion.

Muslims in the United States are sometimes considered "underserved" by insurers and lenders, but it is not clear whether they are underserved because of their religious beliefs, which prohibit the charging of interest, because of their status as immigrants who may not have credit histories in the United States, or because they may not know how to navigate consumer finance. On the one hand, for example, the Department of Insurance of the state of Missouri identifies four groups of residents who often have "slim" credit histories that put them at a disadvantage in applying for insurance or loans: senior citizens, farmers, Hispanics, and Muslims.[4] This might suggest that the religion does play a role. On the other hand, immigrants from majority-Muslim countries do not seem to lack access to home financing when compared with other immigrants. Immigrants from the Caribbean, Central and South America, and Southeast Asia fare far worse than immigrants from South Asia or the Middle East (Papademetriou and Ray 2004). This would suggest that poverty is more important than religion in predicting access to homeownership. The often arbitrary use of racial classifiers makes assessing the current status of Muslim homeownership even more difficult. If people of South Asian and Arab descent are classed as "Asian," for example, then they constitute part of the 55.3 percent of Asians in the United States who own a home, as compared with 43.3 percent of African Americans and 70.5 percent of whites (Papademetriou and Ray 2004, 7). At least one estimate of the rate of homeownership among Muslims in the United States corresponds to the rate for Asians (Thomas 2001, n. 9). The Asian category, of course, also includes groups with very low rates of homeownership, such as Cambodian Americans, and groups with relatively high rates, such as Japanese Americans. Using the Asian category as a best guess to estimate Muslim homeownership, as some industry professionals do, discounts the significant proportion of Muslims who are African American (which may be as high as 42 percent; see Leonard 2003, 4).

At this point, the reader might be inclined to despair. We do not know how many Muslims there are in the United States; we do not know if they have differential access to homeownership; if they do, we do not know if their differential access to homeownership is due to religion, poverty, or slim credit histories caused by neither religion nor poverty. How, then, can we even go about studying the phenomenon of Islamic mortgages?

Such despair would be premature. In exploring the phenomenon of Islamic mortgages, it is helpful to set aside the numbers and rethink the kinds of questions we ask about these mortgages. As I have already suggested, a virtue of anthropological ethnography is that it allows the subjects of research to surprise the researcher and redirect the course of the research. Islamic finance professionals do not talk only about markets; they also talk about dreams—the American dream.

There is no strategic market analysis of the potential for the Islamic mortgage sector in the United States comparable to the one prepared for the United Kingdom by Business Insight.[5] Instead, Islamic mortgages have entered into the public sphere through the rhetoric of the American dream and through the specific provisions of federal programs to make that dream—of homeownership—possible for everyone.[6] Religion and immigration are confounded in this rhetoric. Muslims are identified as "underserved" usually because of religion, but not always. Once the "underserved" designation is made, however, the whole American apparatus of seeking to provide equality of opportunity kicks into gear, together with the idea that with property ownership comes not only citizenship but acculturation. Property, the thinking goes, creates virtuous citizens who care about their neighborhoods, their cities, and their country.

In 1992 Congress passed the Federal Housing Enterprises Financial Safety and Soundness Act (FHEFSSA), which requires greater access to mortgages for lower-income borrowers and spurs innovation in the mortgage sector (Listokin et al. 2001). In 2001 Fannie Mae launched a plan to create "homeownership opportunities" for immigrants by providing education about credit (Fannie Mae Foundation 2001). In 2003 it announced an expansion of its "American Dream Commitment" to finance six million new homeowners—including 1.8 million new minority homeowners—by the year 2014 (Papademetriou and Ray 2004, 1). Instead of being identified as a profitable new niche to exploit, Muslims in the United States have been targets of the apparently altruistic motives of the opportunity society. Indeed, as I demonstrate in this book, Islamic mortgages owe their current expansion, if not their existence, to the ideologies of American opportunity and their instantiation in the institutions that seek to bring those opportunities to all. Islamic mortgages are as much a window into the culture and institutions of the American dream and its specific connection to property ownership as they are into Muslims, Islam, or the relationship between religion and economy.

THE ORGANIZATION OF THE BOOK

In the course of conducting the research that led to this book, I realized that I needed to understand the historical roots of the conventional mortgage if I was to explain the innovations represented by the Islamic version. I would discover, however, that surprisingly little work has been done on the history of the conventional mortgage. For this reason, chapter 1 provides an account of the development of mortgage contracts in the common law. It does so with specific reference to the Christian theological conundrums posed by mortgages during a time when usury was considered sinful. The concept of interest would be gradually separated, however, from that of usury. In the United States, for instance, debates over the potential sinfulness of interest-bearing debt were obviated by the creation of securitized interests in mortgages and the rise of the secondary market. This market had the potential to extend homeownership to everyone, and it also helped very gradually to standardize mortgage law across the various state jurisdictions (a process that is still unfolding). Chapter 1 also reviews the connections between Islamic and Christian injunctions against usury and sets the stage for the development of the Islamic mortgage.

Chapter 2 provides a history of the rise of Islamic mortgages in the United States. It begins with an account of the fortunes of Islamic investing, since a key factor in the growth and development of Islamic mortgages was the decline of the Islamic investment sector after September 11, 2001. Principles developed for Islamic investing were transposed into Islamic home finance and new government partnerships were created after 9/11 to foster the growth of this new Islamic financial service.

Two Islamic mortgage providers are the focus of chapter 3, which compares their models for providing home financing and relates these two models to both medieval Christian debates about mortgages and twentieth-century Islamic debates about the prohibition of interest. One company's model seems on the surface to be more shari'a-compliant than the other's. It has a strong link to an exegetical tradition and uses rent in place of interest. The other model, though based on an administrative fee marked to an interest rate, nevertheless has the support and public backing of prominent shari'a scholars. The differences in the models can be explained by differences in the understanding of shari'a itself. Is shari'a an interpretive activity to be undertaken by pious people in common endeavor? Or is it a practical activity to be carried out under the watchful gaze and supervision of fiqh scholars?

Chapter 4 presents the results of several quantitative analyses of the applicant pools of the two companies discussed in chapter 3. The findings are surprising. Progressive Muslims seem to prefer the model with a clearer exegetical foundation, while more conservative Muslims seem to prefer the model endorsed by prominent scholars. This chapter also paints a picture of the broad characteristics of the client pools of these two lenders in terms of income, race, and geographical location.

Chapter 5 explores the motivations and beliefs of those who seek out Islamic mortgage alternatives. It limns the general discourse about Islamic banking and Islamic mortgages among American Muslims and the broad conversation taking place about the status and nature of Islamic law in the United States. Islam appears more and more in this discourse as a volumetric substance (one can have more or less of it) and as a quality of action (one can "do something Muslim") that is additive to the other aspects of one's existence and identity. Scholarly endorsements warrant one product as "more" shari'a-compliant than another despite people's own misunderstandings of the mechanisms behind those products. Yet scholarly endorsement is not the equivalent of personal charisma. People prefer the greater anonymity afforded by standardized forms, credit checks, and standardized "shari'a seals of approval" over the handshake and the social connections that come from dealing with other Muslims. They want to be treated like "real clients," not just like Muslims.

Chapter 6 discusses the securitization of Islamic mortgages in tradable, mortgage-backed securities. The creation of shari'a-compliant securities is an effort to provide greater liquidity to the American Islamic mortgage market as well as to tap into the wealth of global Muslim investors seeking solid but shari'a-compliant investments backed by American regulatory authorities. It also tracks American Muslims' shifting understandings of the relationship between these globally marketed, mortgage-backed Islamic securities and their own financial investment in their home.

Chapter 7 looks at the relationship between standardization and religious authority. It tracks the work of shari'a supervisory boards in issuing standardized fatwas (jurisprudential rulings) on various Islamic financial products and the role of scholarly authority in creating standards.

The conclusion (chapter 8) revisits the main questions that sparked the research and draws out the book's main arguments about Muslim identity, Islamic mortgages, and the transformation of Islamic law in the United States. What emerges from this study is the extent to which ideas about the anonymity of the market work together with understandings of both professionalism and law to structure the field of Islamic mortgages. People who want an Islamic mortgage also want to be reassured that they are dealing with a legitimate business. Legitimacy is conferred not just by prominent scholars but by the form in which the scholars deliver their opinions and the formality with which an Islamic mortgage company undertakes its activities. The more "legal" things look—the more bureaucratic the paperwork, the more forms and seals and places for signatures, for example—the more a loan-seeking Muslim assumes the transaction is in accordance with "Islamic" law. American popular understandings of what the law is and how it works thus have a profound impact on Muslim Americans' contemporary understanding and assessment of Islamic law in the United States, at least in its instantiation in Islamic financial products like mortgages. It is not so much that property ownership confers cultural citizenship, then, as that a prior legal consciousness demonstrates that one is American through and through.[7]

CHAPTER ONE

WHAT IS A MORTGAGE?
THE HISTORY OF A RELIGIOUS CONCEPT

M ention mortgages and most people's minds turn to homeownership and interest rates. In the early 2000s many Americans may
not have associated mortgages with buying property so much as with
generating extra income by refinancing their existing mortgages and
cashing out the equity they had built up in their house to use for home
improvements or other consumer spending. In 2002 and 2003 combined,
Americans filed almost three times as many applications for refinancing
loans as for conventional mortgages (see table 1.1).

The idea that a mortgage can become a source of wealth for the borrower (the mortgagor) in addition to a source of profit for the lender (the
mortgagee) is the result of a relatively recent historical shift in the understanding of debt, equity, interest, and property. It partly has to do with
the U.S. government policy since the Great Depression of encouraging
homeownership through incentives like the home mortgage interest deduction for federal income taxes: the deductibility of interest on a home
mortgage from reported income for the purpose of figuring yearly income taxes is a prime motivator for many first-time home buyers. This
policy puts renters at a double disadvantage. First, renters never build an
ownership interest in the property on which they live, no matter how
many improvements they might make to it, and second, renters do not
reap the tax benefits of homeownership. Disadvantaging renters often

14

Table 1.1   U.S. Conventional Mortgage and Refinancing Applications, 2002 and 2003

Mortgage Type	Year 2002	Year 2003	Total
Conventional			
Number	4,522,973	5,503,469	10,026,442
Percentage within year	30.1	24.1	26.5
Refinance			
Number	10,480,495	17,286,896	27,767,391
Percentage within year	69.9	75.9	73.5
Total	15,003,468	22,790,365	37,793,833

Source: Author's compilation from Home Mortgage Disclosure Act data.

translates into disadvantages for densely populated urban areas, which often have higher proportions of renters. Scholars and activists have long noted the relationship between the home mortgage interest deduction, the rise of suburbanization, and inner-city blight (see, for example, Jackson 1987; Marshall 2000).

The interest deduction has had other effects as well. In an essay on mortgage interest and government policy, Arthur C. Holden (1966, 105), an architect and planner in New York City, worried that the home mortgage interest deduction would encourage people to maintain rather than reduce their indebtedness and lead borrowers to understand amortization not as the gradual reduction and "killing" of the mortgage debt but as the gradual "increase in the owner's 'investment.'" Indeed, mortgagors today often consult amortization tables not just to figure out when they will fully own their house but to calculate when they will have enough equity built up in it to secure a second loan and "cash out" their investment. Yet amortization itself is an expense, since one has to pay a portion of the loan's principal each month from one's other sources of income. And even a house owned outright, after the complete payment of the mortgage, can be considered a liability, not an asset, since it requires continual additional payments of property taxes, maintenance costs, and so on. A house cannot become an asset unless it is made liquid—hence arguments from financial planners that houses should be placed in a trust (see, for example, Kiyosaki and Lechter 2000). Thus, in a simple household budget, Holden believed, amortization should be considered a liability, not an asset. Holden worried that the home mortgage interest deduction sacrificed long-term stability in the form of freedom from debt for short-term gain; far better, in his opinion, to offer an income tax deduction for the expense of amortization—for paying down the principal—than for the interest.

Holden's essay was little noticed. Yet it contained a peculiar reference to a feudal form of loan called a vif-gage, which Holden saw as morally superior to the mortgage and which I discuss here because it provides insight into contemporary Islamic mortgages. The vif-gage, Holden (1966, 105) wrote, "called for gradual payments for the reduction of the principal of the loan, similar to what we recognize today as amortization"; he underscored the point that "a continuous and understanding reduction of indebtedness is necessary to the maintenance of a stable society." But what was a vif-gage? How did it encourage an "understanding," that is, a conscious reduction of indebtedness? And what kind of contrast was Holden trying to draw between a mortgage and a vif-gage, for does not a mortgage also call for gradual payments reducing the principal of the loan? The answers to these questions reveal the mortgage's *religious* history. The idea that the mortgage can be a source of wealth for the borrower as well as the lender thus involves a shift in notions of property, debt, and interest that are of much longer duration than the twentieth-century U.S. income tax code. This chapter traces that religious genealogy in order to bring into better view the ways in which contemporary American Islamic mortgages both replicate and challenge it. One way to interpret American Islamic mortgages is to see them as retracing the steps of the religious history of conventional mortgages but taking a couple of alternative turns along the way. As I show in the next chapter, this is not an entirely sufficient interpretation. Nevertheless, it helps set the stage for some of the more technical discussions that follow in chapters 2 and 3.

USURY, LIFE, AND DEATH

"Gage, engagement, wage, wages, wager, wed, wedding . . . all spring from one root," wrote Frederick Pollack and Frederic Maitland (1909, 2:117) in their classic *History of English Land Law Before the Time of Edward I.* This root word is the Latin vadium, and it refers to a pledge given as a security against "the payment of money or the performance of some act by the person by whom it was given or from whom it was taken"

(2:118).[1] I pledge my services or my property to you in return for a loan of money you give to me; you are possessed of my pledged property and enjoy my services until I pay off the loan. Pollack and Maitland wrote that gages of land had become common in England during the 1100s; Christians would pledge their land to Jews in return for money to finance the crusades (2:118). The usurious potential of such gages was debated in feudal England. Glanvill's (1998, X:8, 124) twelfth-century treatise on the laws and customs of England distinguished two types of gage based on whether the "profits and rents accruing" from the pledged land "shall count towards repayment." If the profits of the land—its agricultural yield, for example—were used toward repaying the creditor, then the agreement was "just and binding"; if they were not, then the agreement was "unjust and dishonourable, but is not forbidden by the court of the lord king, although it deems it a kind of usury" (124). This second agreement is the mortuum vadium, the "mort-gage" or "dead gage." It is "dead" because the pledged land does not contribute toward the reduction of the debt (Pollack and Maitland 1909, 119). Glanvill never used the term vivum vadium, or "vif-gage," to signify the "living" gage whereby the pledged land did contribute toward reducing the debt from its rents and/or from its living fruits, its yield. Pollack and Maitland noted that the term "vif-gage" did occur in Norman texts but that there was no direct evidence that the vif-gage was ever used in England (119, n. 2). Although the mortgage was permitted, any creditor holding a gaged land under such a "dead pledge" at the time of his death was treated as a usurer—his property was forfeited to the king, and he was considered to have died in sin. According to Glanvill, the usurer was partly forgiven for his sin if he completed the usurious transaction before his death; "but, if he died in the crime, the act had reached the point of criminality—the offence was complete, and the punishment followed" (Osborne 1951/1970, 4, quoting Glanvill 1998, VI:16).

Why was the mort-gage considered a form of usury? There are several competing explanations. One is the Aristotelian argument that money should not beget money, echoed in biblical injunctions against usury (for example, Deuteronomy 23:19, Leviticus 25:36, Luke 6:35) and in other medieval Christian texts. The Old Testament, it should be noted, contains ambivalent passages about the permissibility of the practice; for example, Deuteronomy 23:20 allows that, "unto a stranger thou mayest lend upon usury; but unto thy brother thou shalt not lend upon usury" (see Nelson 1969). The parable of the talents, recounted in Matthew 25, is perhaps one of the more perplexing references to usury in the Christian

Bible, as it seems to endorse the practice as good business sense. The servant who buries his master's silver talents to keep them safe, rather than trade or lend them, is the one who is cast out; the master specifically admonishes him: "You should have put my money to the exchangers, and then at my coming I should have received my own with usury" (Matthew 25:27).

For Aristotle, money's "natural" use was to facilitate trade for the purpose of acquiring the necessities of the household. If, however, the end of such trade was to make more money rather than only what was necessary to supply one's basic needs, then such trade was unnatural, since money here betrayed its inanimate character and took on the qualities of a living thing. It was unjust as well, he noted in *Politics* (I:10), since money was being used to make wealth at the expense of other people. Even if the mort-gage required payments of the land's profits to the creditor, those payments did not decrease the principal of the loan, as in a vif-gage, and thus they were in effect a form of interest.

Another explanation of the usurious nature of the mort-gage is that there is no clear conveyance of a thing to the creditor in return for the loan—only the abstraction of the money payment in the form of interest. Here a transaction is usurious if it is based in something immaterial or intangible (see Holdsworth 1925, 8:105), that is, if it involves intellectus (mind or spirit) without some anterior res (matter or things) backing it. To the medieval Christian, Jesus Christ, the god-man, represented a reconciliation of intellectus and res, a bringing together without remainder of spirit and flesh. As a perfect concordance, Jesus was not a "representation" of God, but God himself, rendered body. Such perfect concordance became the model of truth and justice; representations without anterior backing by something "real" were suspect—in Christendom, they were false gods, since they had not demonstrated the miracle of transubstantiation. Marc Shell (1982, 1995) shows how this problem of representation in Christianity redounded into Western preoccupations with the matter of money—whether money's substance (paper, metal, and so on) can ever be adequate to its transcendental, abstract value. The demand that money *always* be tied to res is one way of sidestepping that preoccupation. By requiring the repayment of the debt's principal through the yield of the land, the vif-gage accomplishes just that. The mort-gage, by contrast, points up the mystery of death itself: what happens to the soul when the body dies? For the believing Christian, there is the promise of life everlasting, but only if one willingly renounces the res of one's own body for the holy body of the living Christ. The usurer seemingly replaces the holy body of Christ with the abstractions of money to achieve everlasting income in the form of interest. This is why if a man died a usurer he was condemned, while if he completed his usurious transactions in his life-time, he might still achieve salvation.

Finally, a mort-gage was considered usurious because the creditor had entered into an arrangement with a borrower without risk: the borrower was obligated to repay the debt, yet the creditor did not assume any risks or obligations in relation to the borrower. In contrast, a vif-gage was based on the fruits of the land, its living products, being channeled into the original loan as repayment. The end of the transaction was life itself (those living fruits), the transaction was backed by the land itself, and the creditor's payments were compensation for his risk in investing in it (Osborne 1951/1970, 4). Medieval Christendom found ways of justifying this compensation in terms of the necessity of making profitable use of one's money and being remunerated for it, like the good servants in the parable of the talents who escape damnation.

It is no mere etymological conceit to linger over the morbid root of mortgages. From their common law beginnings, mortgages were bound up in questions of life, death, sin, and the status of the soul. But shifts in the understanding of death and debt resulted in corresponding shifts in the notions of life and death embedded in such pledges and led to the lack of understanding that Holden complained about in the 1960s.

The first shift had to do with which party to the mortgage encoun-tered the land as "dead," the creditor or the borrower. In the original Glanvillian mortgage, the land was dead to the creditor: he did not re-ceive its fruits. By the late fifteenth century, the time of *Littleton's Tenures*, one of the first law books published in England, a mortgage was understood to be so called because, "if [the debtor] doth not pay, then the land . . . is taken from him for ever, and so [is] dead (to him. . . . And if he doth pay, then the pledge is dead)" (quoted in Osborne 1951/1970, 3).

The second shift had to do with Littleton's parenthetical comment: the gradual elision of the status of the land pledged as living or dead to either the borrower or the lender, and the emphasis on the status of the debt it-self. The debt took precedence over the land securing it. It became the central object whose status as living (active, in process) or dead (com-pleted, amortized) was of utmost concern to both parties. This second shift tracks the transformation of feudal relations based in fiefs, tribute, and living pledges into capitalist relations based on money, commodity exchange, and liquidity. In the latter, the death in the mortgage was oc-cluded by the new emphasis on live and liquid capital. An amortized mortgage was of little conceptual or legal interest because it did not generate any financial interest; it was truly "dead." The only way to understand amortization, then, was as an increase in the borrower's equity, and thus the borrower's potential to enter into new pledges, using that equity to secure more credit and thereby keeping his property liquid—and remaining indebted.

MAKING A (MORAL) MARKET

Ann Burkhart (1999, 259) refers to this shift, beginning in the late sixteenth century, as the "second era" of mortgages. She argues that two legal changes were responsible for bringing it about. The first was the gradual reduction by Parliament of the prohibitions against interest, beginning in 1623 and finally ending in a complete repeal in 1854; the second was the creation of equitable rights in mortgaged land for the borrower. Forfeiture of mortgaged land became less common, and creditors' interest in the land itself diminished as a result. Parliament also restored the franchise to mortgagors in 1696 and gradually recognized the productive uses of loaned money. These legal changes occurred simultaneously with the rise of negotiable instruments—bills of exchange that could be signed over to new bearers and traded in their own right, separate from the tangible assets that ultimately backed them. Making debt negotiable laid the foundation for modern finance, as well as for a secondary market in mortgage loans. While contemporary commentators decried the "fiction" of such financial transactions (see Dugaw 1998; Ingrassia 1998), noting in particular their susceptibility to unscrupulous manipulation (the South Sea Bubble) or frenzied speculation (the Tulip Mania), the usury involved in the new financial system was deemed, if not morally neutral, then a necessary evil whose excesses could be contained. As Sir William Ashley put it, "The moral distinction was tending more and more to become one between excessive demand and moderate demand, rather than between gratuitous and non-gratuitous loan" (quoted in Holdsworth 1925, 8:109). Hence the new distinction between "interest" and "usury": the former is thought of as less morally fraught than the latter, which connotes excess.

In the United States the history of mortgages is somewhat truncated, as Burkhart notes, but follows the general pattern. The chief distinction is that American mortgage law "evolved more quickly than English law to focus on the debt aspect of the mortgage relationship" (Burkhart 1999, 267). In addition, owing to the patchwork of regulatory and legal environments created by separate state legislative frameworks, mortgage law is not uniform throughout the United States. Title-theory states grant the lender the "immediate right to possess the mortgaged land," because the mortgage conveys the title to the land to the lender (267).[2] Lien-theory states, by contrast, treat the mortgage as a lien against the land and thus do not permit the lender to take immediate possession. In lien-theory, the mortgage is understood to be only a security against the loan—a mort-gage. Lenders have no other interest in it and do not seek its fruits; should the borrower default, lenders want to off-load it as soon as possible. The real profit comes from the trade of negotiable instruments, not the enjoyment of the real property.

The growth of the secondary market in mortgage paper has had a number of important effects. First, consider the relationship between intellectus and res. As the focus of the mortgage becomes the debt and not the property, it becomes possible to mortgage property in advance of its being owned. In a conventional mortgage today the borrower probably does not yet own any real property. The aim of the mortgage for the borrower is to acquire some. The borrower in effect pledges a house he or she does not yet own as the security against the loan, which in turn is used to finance the purchase of the same house. It is a double contract, the first half of which is an act of faith based on credit histories; credit, etymologically, is derived from the Latin verb credere, to trust or believe. These histories of belief or faith then secure the second half of the contract. The mortgage is an act of faith twice over—first, that the borrower has credit, and second, that the real property secures the debt. The latter attempts to sidestep the problem of the relationship between money (intellectus) and tangible property (res) by attaching the one to the other, but the former takes on the metaphysical character of judging the borrower's soul (while leaving that of the lender hidden from view).

Securitizing mortgages—bundling them together and creating salable shares in them on the secondary market—adds another level of abstraction. The mortgage, an abstraction from the property based on the borrower's credit, is further abstracted from the property and made partible or divisible into abstract units that can be disaggregated and reaggregated at will into new bundles that can be purchased by others (or further divided into shares and repackaged into other bundles, and so on). The net result is to remove the physical property ever further from the lender.

So what? First, the growth of the secondary market insulates lenders from the risk of any one individual default. It allows them to spread the risk of issuing mortgages. In the United States after the Great Depression, Congress created the Federal Housing Administration (FHA, 1934) to insure mortgages and the Federal National Mortgage Association (FNMA, or Fannie Mae, 1938) to purchase FHA loans and sell them on the secondary market. This began a process of government-sponsored enterprise (GSE) dominance in the secondary mortgage market, which has been credited with creating a nation of homeowners. In 1968 Congress split FNMA into two parts: the Government National Mortgage Association (GNMA, or Ginnie Mae) retains the function of backing FHA and Veterans Administration (VA) loans, and Fannie Mae is a privately owned GSE that can purchase and resell any mortgages, even those not guaranteed by an insurer or federal agency. To further spur the flow of capital into the housing market, Congress passed the Emergency Home Finance Act (1970), which created the Federal Home Loan Mortgage Corporation (FHLMC, or Freddie Mac). Freddie Mac purchases and resells conventional home mortgages. The commercial mortgage market was opened up in the 1980s (see Burkhart 1999, 273–76).

Second, the rise of the secondary market freed lenders from geographical and personal or community constraints. The mortgage market increasingly had little to do with the residential properties of any particular area. Lenders "traditionally made loans based on the security of land located within fifty miles of their office" (Burkhart 1999, 271). This practice in part "reflected the essentially personal character of the relationship between borrower and lender." This personal relationship was "shattered" by the secondary mortgage market (272). Now a lender might not even look at a photograph of the mortgaged property (279). The mortgage market also increasingly has had little to do with the actual person of the borrower; instead of "relying on personal evaluations," the lender now relies on credit ratings (278). The result is an increasingly anonymized market. Borrowers are often surprised when their lender sells their loan, often within a few months of its commencement, or when they see their credit scores for the first time.

The Community Reinvestment Act (CRA) of 1977 sought to repersonalize lending by requiring lenders to serve the needs of the communities in which they operated. The CRA sought to eliminate "redlining," by which banks would refuse to lend within regions coterminous with racial and ethnic minorities and/or a high proportion of residents living in or near poverty. But the existence of a national secondary mortgage market and the gradual relaxation of restrictions on lenders who fail to comply with the CRA have further anonymized the market. As one commentator notes, "The secondary market is like a great food processor. What goes in comes out unrecognizable to borrowers and lenders, but looks appetizing to investors. The raw material in the process, the mortgage itself, is now incidental to the process" (quoted in Burkhart 1999, 272).

The anonymous and highly abstracted market of mortgage-backed securities does serve one of its stated functions: it generates capital that gets invested into the housing sector, and it reduces the cost of American mortgages. According to the Freddie Mac website in 2003:

> Just as stock and bond markets have put investor capital to work for corporations, the secondary mortgage market puts private investor capital to work for homebuyers and apartment owners, providing a continuous flow of affordable funds for home financing. We like to call it "linking Main Street with Wall Street."

And taken in its religious and historical context, the secondary mortgage market illustrates the nineteenth-century philosopher Georg Simmel's (1907/1990) argument that modern money, by anonymizing transactions, frees people from potentially onerous social ties. Simmel had in mind the old tributary, feudal ties, but he also found democratic potential in modern money's abstraction and detachment from community and real property.

The creation of a secondary market has had another important effect in the United States. Because different states have different laws, and because "mortgage law has never been thoroughly overhauled and modernized," this market remains relatively unstandardized or rationalized. The participation of federally sponsored agencies in the secondary market, however, has brought increasing standardization (Burkhart 2002, 571).

It is not surprising that critics of the modern mortgage market invoke the rhetoric and argumentation of the feudal religious injunctions against usury and also attempt to create solutions to the problems caused by modern mortgages using those same tools. The opposition between personalization and standardization reflects an opposition between social relations and the abstraction of the market, as well as between the tangibility of property and the transcendent value that it supposedly animates (or that animates it). Burkhart (1999) notes a "third stage" of mortgage law that attempts to hold the lender accountable for particular deficiencies or dangers of the property held in security against the loan—in particular, for environmental problems on the land or for the uses of the land for criminal purposes. Here, requiring the lender to take an interest in the potentially destructive activities occurring on the mortgaged land or its environmental liabilities reinforces a relationship between the lender and the pledged land. Lenders are thus enlisted in a moral project: since "virtually every parcel of privately owned land is mortgaged at some time, lenders are uniquely situated to help implement government programs at little or no cost to the government. . . . The hallmark of the third era [of mortgage law] may prove to be the law's increasing burdens for lenders to further the public good" (Burkhart 1999, 314).

SETTING THE STAGE FOR THE ISLAMIC MORTGAGE

The medieval Christian injunctions against usury are echoed in contemporary Islamic financial practice, although there is considerable debate over whether the Qur'anic term "riba," designating increase, can be simply translated as "interest" and/or "usury." All three arguments against the usurious nature of the mort-gage in medieval England can be found in contemporary Islamic banking and finance. The Aristotelian objection to money's fecundity is found in the statement of the Pasadena, California–based American Finance House—LARIBA about its organizing concepts: "Money is not a commodity. It is a measuring scale. It also does not reproduce. It only grows when used in an economic activity. Money is man-made."[3] American Finance House—LARIBA was one of the earliest entrants into the Islamic mortgage market. The concern that a contract should be clearly bound to a physical, tangible asset is found in the *Guide to Understanding Islamic Home Finance in Accordance with Islamic Shari'ah*, a booklet introduced by Shaykh Yusuf Talal DeLorenzo, who sits on the shari'a supervisory board of the Guidance Financial Group and other Islamic financial service companies; he offers this explanation:

A conventional mortgage loan is a loan of money secured by a lien against property. A *halal* [lawful, Islamically acceptable] home acquisition agreement, on the other hand, is either a partnership in property, a loan of property, or a sale of property. In other words, the essential difference between a Shari'ah-compliant method of home finance and a conventional loan is the difference between:

- An acceptable transaction that involves acquiring something of tangible value—in this case, real estate—for cash.

- An unacceptable transaction that involves borrowing cash and promising to repay that cash plus an added amount. (Morris and Thomas 2002, 3, italics in original)

The concern that the lender should not be insulated from the risks of business is found throughout the Islamic banking literature (see Vogel and Hayes 1998) and is embedded in the profit-and-loss-sharing contracts that animate a good deal of Islamic financial activity (see Maurer 2005). The American Finance House—LARIBA mortgage model explicitly invokes risk-sharing, as discussed in the next chapter.

Islamic banking and finance begins from the Qur'anic injunctions against riba. Riba, literally "increase," often translated as "usury" or "interest," occurs twenty times in the Qur'an. Five verses in particular stand out:

> Those that live on usury [riba] shall rise up before God like men whom Satan has demented by his touch; for they claim that trading is no different from usury. But God has permitted trading and made usury unlawful. He that has received an admonition from his Lord and mended his ways may keep his previous gains; God will be his judge. Those that turn back [turn again to riba] shall be the inmates of the Fire, wherein they shall abide for ever. (2:275)

> God has laid His curse on usury and blessed almsgiving with increase [yurbi, root: RaBa]. God bears no love for the impious and the sinful. (2:276)

> Believers, have fear of God and waive what is still due to you from usury, if your faith be true, or war shall be declared against you by God and his apostle. If you repent, you may retain your principal, suffering no loss and causing loss to none. (2:278–79)

> Believers, do not live on usury, doubling your wealth many times over. Have fear of God, that you may prosper. (3:130)

> That which you seek to increase by usury will not be blessed by God; but the alms you give for His sake shall be repaid to you many times over. (30:39)[+]

The last verse brings two forms of increase together so that they cancel each other out: riba and alms (also, literally, "increase").

Islamic banking and finance consists of experiments taking place around the world to create financial products and banking institutions that do not rely on interest. Much of the activity is taking place in Malaysia, Indonesia, the United States, the United Kingdom, the Arabian peninsula, the Indian subcontinent, and, to a lesser extent, west and east Africa. In other words, this activity has not just taken place within the financial systems of nation-states that have officially at one time or another "Islamized" their economies, such as the Sudan, Brunei, Iran, and Pakistan. The broadest definition of Islamic banking and finance includes all activities understood to be financial or economic that seek to avoid riba—itself a term of considerable definitional anxiety—generally through profit-and-loss sharing, leasing, or other forms of equity- or asset-based financing.

As I have discussed elsewhere (for example, Maurer 2005), global Islamic banking today owes much to the immigration of Middle Eastern and South Asian students and professionals to the United States and the United Kingdom during the 1970s and 1980s and the consolidation of large U.S. Muslim organizations such as the Islamic Society of North America and the Islamic Circle of North America. The oil boom in the Middle East during the 1970s, which sparked renewed interest in Islamic banking in many Muslim-majority countries (see, for example, Warde 2000, 92–93; Wilson 1990), also encouraged the development of a loose-knit, interconnected network of Muslim international businessmen who, working for oil and chemical companies as well as financial firms, gained experience in Western regulatory and business environments. The main nodes of this network were the financial and industrial centers of Europe and the United States, not the Middle East or South Asia. Since 2000 or 2001, repatriated businessmen and bankers in the Gulf states have made significant efforts to re-center the field of Islamic banking in the Middle East, particularly Bahrain and Dubai, by hosting major international conferences and other activities. Nevertheless, some of the main sites for intellectual production in Islamic economics are places like the Institute of Islamic Banking and Insurance in London and the Harvard Islamic Finance Information Program in Cambridge, Massachusetts. Despite the new emergence of centers of Islamic banking intellectual activity and actual practice in the Gulf, those who now promote their approaches to the field and their products in the Middle East or, to a lesser extent, in Pakistan owe much of their fame to their diasporic connections or the international authority they have acquired through their travels in the West.

Mahmoud El-Gamal (2000a, 146–47), an influential economist who has written extensively on Islamic banking, notes with both amusement and concern that Islamic banking tends to use Arabic terms for its contractual forms when perfectly acceptable English translations are available, while it lackadaisically translates "riba" as "interest" or "usury" despite the lack of an adequate translation. For El-Gamal, it should be noted, none of the three Christian objections to usury map onto corresponding Islamic ones so easily. To him, the Islamic prohibition against riba is meant to protect against market inefficiencies and protect us from our irrational natures and bad choices (see El-Gamal 1999). In another work (Maurer 2005), I have argued that perhaps Islamic banking should be viewed not simply as the implementation of Qur'anic prohibitions against riba but as the debate over riba itself.

For the purposes of the present volume, however, I would simply point out that the late-twentieth-century invention of Islamic mortgages in the United States replicates the historical and religious development of the mortgage but inflects it through Islamic finance debates over the nature and status of riba. Those debates do crop up in the field of Islamic mortgages, since companies may claim that their competitors' products do not strictly or properly adhere to the prohibition, as we see in the next chapter.

To return to the history of conventional mortgages, it is ironic that the countervailing tendencies in conventional mortgage law—its unrationalized and patchwork, decentralized qualities, on the one hand, and its increasing standardization through the activities of federally sponsored agencies like Freddie Mac, on the other—are the conditions that make Islamic mortgages possible in the United States. That which is not fully "rational" is also open to experimentation; having a patchwork of different kinds of mortgage regimes gives professionals the flexibility to craft an Islamically permissible product. These conditions also leave the door open to sacred meanings and motivations for mortgages, since not being fully rational can entail not being fully secular either (to the extent that the conventional mortgage was ever fully secularized). Meanwhile, national standardization that transcends local particularities mirrors the umma, or world community of Muslims, which transcends local cultural differences or traditions. National standards can protect minority populations as well, since at least in theory such standards must account for the whole nation rather than only a specific locale or interest group and must serve the nation uniformly. Thus, federally sponsored enterprises involved in the mortgage sector have had an obligation to extend homeownership opportunities to underserved populations, including Muslims. Indeed, federally sponsored enterprises like Freddie Mac, as we will see, have proved instrumental in spurring the growth of Islamic mortgages in the United States.

CHAPTER TWO

WHAT IS AN ISLAMIC MORTGAGE?

In the aftermath of the attacks of September 11, 2001, Islamic banking came under the scrutiny of the Federal Bureau of Investigation (FBI), the Department of Treasury, and other U.S. government agencies that sought to track and interdict financial transactions that might be linked to global terrorism. The news media quickly generated reports about Islamic charities potentially posing as front organizations for money laundering or terrorist fund-raising, and traditional informal credit associations, like hawala, also suddenly came under suspicion.[1] Where just months earlier the mainstream media had promoted the virtues of Islamic banking in a series of newspaper reports and television spots about new interest-free mortgage alternatives for Muslims, suddenly the reports focused on the shady and illicit.[2] Now Islamic financial alternatives were reported as having less to do with religious injunctions against interest than with clandestine and possibly criminal financial activities.

Surprisingly, however, Islamic banking in the United States underwent considerable growth and expansion after September 11, 2001. In particular, home financing, which many people I interviewed told me was the cornerstone of the "American dream," has achieved considerable national prominence on the American Islamic banking scene. This chapter attempts to explain why, compared to other countries' experiences with Islamic banking, mortgage financing has taken on such prominence in American Islamic banking. It also reviews the history of American Islamic mortgage products and reflects on the convergence between the role of interpretation in Islamic jurisprudence and in U.S. banking regulation—a convergence that permits Islamic mortgage experimentation and also muddles the distinctions between conventional and Islamic mortgage products.

THE AFTERMATH OF 9/11 AND OTHER FINANCIAL CRISES

"Everyone collectively began to hold their breath." These words, from an Islamic banking specialist in Islamic law, sum up the response of the professionals I interviewed about the impact of terrorist attacks of September 11 on the industry. Like other Americans and people around the world, this professional felt that the events of September 11 had introduced a previously unimaginable degree of generalized insecurity and instability, especially for American Muslims. For Islamic banking, the effects were twofold. First, the suspension of trading in the U.S. stock exchanges, the shock to world markets, the withdrawal of investment capital from U.S. markets, and the lack of confidence in the future had a dramatic impact on all financial and investment activity, including Islamic banking. Second, the immediate assumption that international terrorists professing the Islamic faith were responsible for the attacks cast a chill over American Muslims and created fears of government reprisals against all Muslims—a "witch-hunt," in the words of one interviewee. The rounding up and detention of American Muslims and immigrants without due process, the freezing of the assets of several Muslim charities, the hate crimes against Muslim individuals and institutions, and the pronouncements of prominent politicians and opinion leaders that Islam itself was to blame lent credence to these concerns, which were not mollified by the conciliatory and inclusive gestures offered by some government leaders and the media. Where previously Muslims might have worried about anti-Muslim hate crimes committed by individuals or anti-Muslim rhetoric from certain evangelical Christian leaders, now, in addition, "public policy became a factor and public policy became a fear," as one interviewee put it.

Because of the fear that public policy would now target Muslims, many clients of Islamic banking businesses began to withdraw their money and commitment. Interviewees were quick to point out that this reaction, together with a wait-and-see attitude, prevailed not only among clients of Islamic finance businesses but among investors of all stripes. But the prevailing cautiousness took on a particular character for Muslims: "It was kind of a minefield," one interviewee said, especially as those charged with tracing terrorist money began to freeze the assets of Muslim charities. At the same time, most people I interviewed expressed confidence that regulatory agencies "knew about the entities they were dealing with" and that investigators had quickly begun to appreciate the difference between terrorist financing and Islamic financing. Still, many worried that the fears of many American Muslims were not being quelled but in fact stoked by politically driven anti-Muslim rhetoric. Nearly all interviewees noted a renewed anti-Islam discourse, especially among evangelical Christian leaders like Rev. Franklin Graham, as the primary challenge facing Muslims in American society.

Of course, the events of September 11 are only part of the story of what has happened in Islamic banking since that date. Almost as significant—and to some interviewees more significant—has been the crisis in confidence in corporations brought on by the accounting scandals of the early 2000s and the bursting of the stock market bubble in the spring of 2002. The year 2002 was a bad one for financial services and investment all around, and not surprisingly, Islamic banking professionals reacted by heavily emphasizing the need for greater accountability and transparency in corporate activities. The new attention given to audit and accounting procedures, they believed, stood to help Islamic banking and finance in the long run. New initiatives (such as that of the Bahrain-based Accounting and Auditing Organization for Islamic Financial Institutions, or AAOIFI) generated interest in the United States and abroad and even helped spark outreach and education efforts on Islamic banking at the highest levels of government. After returning from a trip to Bahrain, where he met with the head of the AAOIFI, former Secretary of the Treasury Paul O'Neill directed his undersecretary for international affairs, John B. Taylor, to issue a call for a seminar titled "Islamic Finance 101." Held on April 26, 2002, in Washington, D.C., the seminar attracted over one hundred participants from various government agencies (Treasury, State, and others) and congressional offices who spent the day learning the fundamentals of Islamic finance from some of the field's leading specialists. The charge of the seminar, as Taylor put it, was to "demystify Islamic banking for our colleagues in Washington who may not have had exposure to this topic."[3] Although the seminar was considered a "very positive experience" by those who attended, others viewed Treasury's effort as a weak response to the freezing of assets of charities and a perceived lack of transparency and accountability regarding the U.S. government's own actions in counterterrorism since September 11.[4]

It is necessary to understand the changing fortunes of Islamic investing in order to appreciate the remarkable resilience and expansion of Islamic home finance since September 11, 2001. The next two sections summarize the post-9/11 issues specific to Islamic investing; the final section covers issues specific to Islamic lending.

ISLAMIC INVESTING

Several companies have been offering Islamic investment vehicles, such as mutual funds, in the United States since the late 1980s. Because Islam prohibits certain kinds of business activities (those that deal with pork, alcohol, gambling, pornography, and, according to some interpretations, arms production and tobacco, among others), an Islamic mutual fund manager seeking to create a portfolio must first screen out companies that engage in religiously forbidden activities. Because Islam prohibits interest or usury, financial service companies must also be screened out of the investable universe. Many corporations engage in a wide range of activities not linked to their primary business (hotels serve alcohol, for instance, and General Motors offers credit cards), and those whose secondary activities violate Islamic law are screened out as well. Owing to the prohibition of interest, Islamic portfolio managers have also developed screens based on the financial standing and financial activities of companies that offer stock. The first excludes companies whose debt-to-market capitalization ratio is greater than or equal to 33 percent. The second excludes companies whose ratio of accounts receivables to total assets is greater than or equal to 45 percent. The third excludes companies whose interest income is greater than one-third of its market capitalization.[5]

Such screening, however, poses a problem for Islamic investing, a problem that may seem esoteric to the outside observer but becomes crucially important for the maintenance of Islamic funds' "Islamic-ness": how to deal with that proportion of earnings that ultimately derives from the percentage of a corporation's activity that is based on interest or interest-bearing debt. Financial ratio screens do not eliminate these earnings entirely but keep them within certain limits. To solve this problem Islamic investing has devised "purification" techniques that catch the proportion of earnings ultimately derived from interest and debt and filter them out of a fund's total earnings. Once the amount of "tainted" revenue is calculated (itself a complicated process), it is deducted from the fund's dividends and given to charity in the form of a gift (usually understood to be a form of voluntary alms, or sadaqa, not zakat, the religiously mandated alms required of all Muslims who are able to pay). Islamic investment companies have traditionally purified their funds by donating most tainted revenues to various Islamic charities. After September 11, this practice came under scrutiny. As one professional put it to me in an interview, "New revelations were coming up every day, and I guess for whatever reason these charities make ideal fronts, but, I mean, who'd a thunk it?" "Guilt by association" also figured in the regulatory and investigative efforts to trace terrorist money after September 11, and "a lot of fingers were being pointed." What had made Islamic investing unique, and uniquely Islamic, suddenly became suspect. For American Muslims and others who had invested in Islamic mutual funds, the link between portfolio purification and Islamic charities led many to reconsider their investments, mainly out of the fear of being investigated, harassed, or tarred with the same brush as terrorist financing. A year after September 11, 2001, one investment professional stated that, in his view, "things are improved, but not restored."

At the same time, once the immediate fears faded, the stock market crash further dampened Islamic investors' enthusiasm. Movements in the Islamic investment market and the stock market were closely correlated. The screens employed in Islamic investing tend to favor technology and blue-chip stocks, and such stocks were among the hardest hit in the market downturn of 2002. For example, the performance of the Amana Growth Fund and the Islamic Market Index Growth Fund mirrored that of the larger market. The accounting scandals and allegations of corporate malfeasance that drew many investors away from the market also hurt Islamic investing. Like other Americans, American Muslims who had invested in the stock market began to take their money out and put it into alternatives. Of particular interest here is the turn toward real estate.

Islamic investment professionals after September 11 also sought to identify their products and services as "ethical," "socially responsible," or "faith-based" financial services, rather than relying solely on the "Islamic" label. Indeed, many Islamic banking professionals I interviewed mentioned this shift in strategy, although for some it was simply a logical outgrowth of their pre-9/11 activities and the preexisting categorization of Islamic investing by the business press and marketing research agencies as part of the "socially responsible" and "ethical" banking and investment family. Still, some professionals have explicitly stressed that Islamic investing is a form of ethical or socially responsible investing, and others have briefly explored using categories and labels such as "Abrahamic." The "faith-based" label, though perhaps the most obvious, seems to have less purchase, however, than "ethical" or "socially responsible." This may be because the "faith-based" umbrella brings together members of some religious constituencies, such as evangelical Christians, who have been openly hostile to Muslims and Islam. Professionals explain the similarity to socially responsible funds by invoking the (often imaginary) connection between Islamic banking and community development, as well as the similarities between the screening mechanisms of Islamic and socially responsible funds. Some cite with approval Domini Social Investments, which manages the largest socially and environmentally screened index fund. Some Islamic finance professionals' personal and professional networks extend to current and former employees of Domini. None, however, ever mentioned the Timothy Plan funds or any other similar mutual funds targeted to very conservative Christians.[6]

Like other investment fund companies, Islamic funds in the wake of the stock market downturn began to stress long-term savings over short-term growth. In an effort to convince investors to return to the market and stay in over the long term instead of worrying about short-term fluctuations of volatile markets, they emphasized retirement funds, college savings funds, and the like. Home financing was seen by industry professionals as a part of this broader move toward stability and the long term.

THE ORIGINS OF AMERICAN ISLAMIC HOME FINANCE

The American Finance House—LARIBA (hereafter "American Finance House") wrote the first "Islamic mortgage" in 1987 for the purchase of a home in Madison, Wisconsin (see Abdul-Rahman and Abdelaaty 2000; Abdul-Rahman and Tug 1999; Ebrahim and Hasan 1993). The mortgage contract followed a cost-plus model (murabaha),[7] according to which the finance house purchased the house and the client paid the cost of the house plus a preset and unchanging markup over a period of time. It was the preset and unchanging amount of the markup that distinguished this contract from a conventional interest-based mortgage, from the point of view of Islamic finance. Later mortgage products developed by American Finance House used lease-to-purchase agreements based on ijara, or leasing contracts from classical Islamic jurisprudence.

Two Middle Eastern financial companies had attempted to offer Islamic financial services in the United States as well, but with limited success, as did a small financial services company based in Houston, Texas. The Saudi firm Dallah al-Baraka opened a subsidiary in California in 1988, only to move to Chicago shortly thereafter and shift its emphasis from consumer finance to real estate and industrial investment. The United Bank of Kuwait (UBK) opened a mortgage company, al-Manzil, in 1998, but closed shop in 2000. In its two years of operation it provided loans for sixty households. The Ameen Housing Cooperative in Palo Alto, California, has been helping Muslims buy homes using ijara contracts since 1998. MSI, an outgrowth of the Islamic Circle of North America, offered various loan products to consumers based on lease-to-purchase and co-ownership models in the Houston area, but never achieved the visibility or scale of American Finance House. Unlike MSI and American Finance House, UBK and al-Baraka lacked a constituency in the communities in which they attempted to operate; as a result, they could not mobilize the networks into which the other two companies had tapped through community connections, mosques, and political and social organizations. Significantly, however, UBK's brief foray into Islamic home finance sparked an interpretive ruling from the Office of the Comptroller of the Currency (OCC) that has had enduring significance for the field (discussed later in the chapter).

In March 2001, Freddie Mac signaled its support for American Finance House's Islamic mortgages by investing $1 million in existing American Finance House contracts. It has since invested a total of $45 million. Freddie Mac support has been hailed as an incredible milestone in the growing visibility and legitimacy of Islamic mortgage alternatives. Before September 11, Freddie Mac had begun to expand its purchase of Islamic mortgage alternatives. In August 2001, it invested $10 million to purchase lease contracts from Standard Federal Bank and United Mortgage of America in Detroit.[8] Freddie Mac support has been crucial to the success and expansion of the Islamic mortgage alternative sector. In 2003 Fannie Mae agreed to purchase $10 million in Islamic financing contracts.[9]

Since Freddie Mac got involved in Islamic home finance, Islamic and conventional banks have devised a number of new home financing options for American Muslims. The most significant new entrant into the field is Guidance Financial, incorporated in 2002, which entered into an agreement with Freddie Mac for an initial commitment of $200 million.[10] It quickly established a national reach and has emerged as American Finance House's chief competitor nationally. The multinational bank

HSBC (formerly the Hong Kong and Shanghai Banking Corporation) opened its "Amanah" Islamic finance window in 2003–2004 and began offering a home finance product based on the murabaha contract. In 2004 SHAPE devised a lease-to-own homeownership program that it calls MALT™ (Mortgage Alternative Loan Transaction), based on an ijara contract; it offers a mortgage-alternative calculator on its webpage (www.shapefinancial.com) so that potential borrowers can compare its product with a conventional mortgage. In 2004 University Bank in Michigan hired a specialist in Islamic mortgage financing to implement the MALT™ model under its community banking division.[11] In Minnesota the Federal Reserve Bank of Minneapolis, seeking a way to serve the financial needs of Somali Muslim immigrants, began exploring home financing alternatives together with a consultancy firm called Reba-Free, the St. Paul Neighborhood Development Center, the Northside Residents Redevelopment Council, and other community organizations (Bennett and Foster 2002; Minnesota Housing Finance Authority 2002, 9; Tyndall 2001). The Neighborhood Development Center began offering both murabaha- and ijara-based mortgage alternatives for business financing. Devon Bank in Chicago also began offering murabaha- and ijara-based mortgage alternatives in 2003. Table 2.1 presents an overview of the various contractual forms that have been used for Islamic mortgage alternatives in comparison with a conventional mortgage. Table 2.2 presents hypothetical payment schedules for a conventional mortgage, an ijara-based mortgage alternative, and a diminishing musharaka-based mortgage alternative.

After digesting the models and the figures, readers may wonder, "Well, what's the real difference between Islamic mortgages and conventional ones? The payments are similarly structured, and the numbers work out pretty much the same even if the components are called by other names or set by other criteria." This is a key question for Islamic banking professionals and potential clients as well. In fact, they debate it endlessly, and that debate may be more important than the actual products. I return to this point at the end of the chapter.

The new entrants into the field of Islamic home finance have helped to address one of the chief shortcomings of Islamic mortgage alternatives: long waiting lists for financing. Prior to Freddie Mac and Fannie Mae, potential clients sometimes waited as long as five or six years to get an Islamic mortgage, since the lender's capital was bound up in its currently held properties and could not attract depositors without violating the separation of commercial from investment banking that was mandated by

TABLE 2.1   Comparison of Home Finance Contractual Forms

Form	Contractual Type	Terms
Conventional mortgage	Interest-bearing loan	Borrower pays the principal plus interest each month according to an amortization schedule. Payment amount stays constant, but an increasing proportion of the payment is put toward the principal of the loan over time.
Murabaha	Cost-plus	Borrower pays a preset and unchanging fraction of the total loan amount ("principal") plus a preset and unchanging markup each month ("fee").
Ijara	Lease	Borrower pays the principal plus a portion of the fair market rent of the property determined by the borrower's share of ownership, which increases with each monthly payment, thereby decreasing the portion of the rent paid to the lender.
Diminishing musharaka	Partnership	Borrower and lender enter into a corporate partnership that owns the property. Borrower buys out the lender's shares in the partnership over time ("ownership payment" or "acquisition payment," structurally similar to principal) plus a "profit payment" to the lender as an administrative fee (structurally similar to an interest payment).

Source: Author's compilation.

TABLE 2.2 Comparing Mortgage and Mortgage-Replacement Product Payments: A Hypothetical Example

| | Payment 1 | | | Payment 2 | | | | | Interest, Rent, or Profit as a Percentage of Principal |
	Principal Payment	Interest or Interest Alternative	Total Monthly Payment	Principal Payment	Interest or Interest Alternative	Total Monthly Payment	Total Repaid	Total Interest, Rent, or Profit Payment	
Conventional mortgage	$448.95	$500.00	$948.95	$450.82	$498.13	$948.95	$170,811.63	$50,811.63	42.3
Ijara mortgage	346.78	800.00	1,146.78	349.09	797.69	1,146.78	206,421.27	86,421.27	72.0
Diminishing musharaka mortgage	448.95	500.00	948.95	450.82	498.13	948.95	170,811.63	50,811.63	42.3

Source: Author's compilation.

Note: First two payments and payment summary for a $150,000 (U.S. dollars) house purchased with 20 percent down payment (loan amount = $120,000) for a fifteen-year term of loan or contract. Conventional mortgage interest rate = 5 percent; ijara monthly rent = $1,000; diminishing musharaka profit payment = 5 percent (market estimates from June 2005). Note that the payment structure and summaries for the ijara contract are equivalent to those for a conventional fifteen-year fixed-rate mortgage at 8 percent.

national banking laws until the 1999 Financial Services Modernization Act.[12] Furthermore, the National Bank Act and state-by-state banking charters generally treat mortgages as liens against the collateral of the property rather than as the actual holding of the title to the property (see Bennett, Foster, and Tyndall 2002).

For Freddie Mac, investing in Islamic mortgage alternatives fell under its mandate to expand opportunities for underserved populations to gain access to homeownership.[13] Freddie Mac's commitment has endured, unchanged, since September 11, 2001. Indeed, according to one interviewee, the only change brought about by September 11 has been "a new sense of resolve that what we're working on is more important now than it was on 9/10." Indeed, Islamic financial institutions offering mortgage alternatives have seen an increase in business and inquiries since 2001. Some attribute this increase to the general turn away from the stock market and into real estate. Others, however, attribute it to a feeling that American Muslims after September 11 want more than ever to assert their position as full members of American society. They also see homeownership affecting the political evolution of American Muslims. As one remarked:

> The most intangible thing is that, when you take puritan Muslims who refuse to participate in interest, and have lived in apartments and so on, and put them in decent neighborhoods, they will start mixing with the American community and become responsible American citizens, and this will grow in the neighborhoods and develop relationships and friendships and so forth.

In addition, both Islamic and conventional banking professionals see incredible economic potential in home financing alternatives:

> At this point we're dealing with a sleeping giant. But . . . it's about to hit in a big way. And the reason for that is the appearance very shortly of home acquisition programs. . . . The home acquisition programs . . . address an essential need, and they basically put something in people's pockets, whereas the other programs—I mean the investment things, the different funds that are developed—those are either aimed at high-net-worth individuals or institutions or, at the retail level, they're for people with *extra* money.

The role of Freddie Mac cannot be understated. Freddie Mac also spurred the Islamic home financing community to begin to conceptualize the securitization of Islamic mortgage alternatives for the purpose of selling Islamic mortgage paper on the secondary market to investors seeking Islamically acceptable investment vehicles. An interviewee remarked that this creates an incentive for "organizations with the deep pockets" to step in. Securitization also makes Islamic mortgage alternatives scalable in a way they had not been before, when they were primarily local or regional affairs backed by small investors. This aspect of Islamic home finance is discussed in chapter 6.

In addition to providing liquidity, stability, and scalability, the support of Freddie Mac generated competition among Islamic financial service providers. Islamic banking professionals pride themselves on their civility, collegiality, and the spirit of cooperation, mutual trust, and inquisitive experimentation that underpins their activities. When heated, debates are usually conducted privately, and they tend to occur over very technical matters of the interpretation of fiqh, or jurisprudence. Since 2002, however, Islamic banking and finance has taken on some of the qualities associated with other forms of competitive enterprise. Professionals market their products and emphasize the benefits (financial, spiritual, or otherwise) of their products over those of their competitors. There has also been increasing market differentiation and fragmentation, with different products being marketed to different communities of Muslims. These developments are discussed further in chapters 4 and 5.

IJTIHAD

As mentioned earlier, when the United Bank of Kuwait attempted to offer home financing alternatives for Muslims in New York, its most enduring legacy was the interpretive ruling its efforts generated from the Office of the Comptroller of the Currency. The OCC regulates banks and financial companies in the United States and issues rulings on matters of legal or regulatory interpretation. In its Interpretive Letter 806, issued in 1997, the OCC accepted UBK's "net leasing" program as a form of financing rather than leasing, because it was "functionally equivalent to or a logical outgrowth of secured lending" (OCC 806, 4). In 1999 OCC Interpretive Letter 867 scripted a murabaha cost-plus contract into its existing understanding of the National Bank Act's sections 24 and 29.[14]

What is significant here is neither the incorporation of an "Islamic" contractual form into "conventional" regulations nor the encompassment or containment of the "Islamic" form by the "conventional," but rather their entanglements. From the Islamic banking perspective, the interpretive letter can be seen as a manifestation of ijtihad, or scriptural interpretation, and thus as divine inspiration working through the minds of human beings seeking routes to the one truth of God. From the regulatory perspective, murabaha is just another kind of contract and can be added to the laundry list of contractual forms and techniques that set in motion the proprietary procedures of a desacralized modernity.

Yet in a sense neither can proceed without the other. Islamic banking and finance needs the interpretive letter to warrant its own ijtihad. Without the ruling, Islamic banking and finance simply could not proceed as easily in the U.S. regulatory landscape. The OCC underwrites Islamic bankers' interpretive activity. At the same time, the OCC proceeds by analogy to banks' other lending activities. In this, it engages in a hermeneutic or interpretive procedure similar to the Islamic jurisprudential technique of qiyas, or reasoning by analogy. From an Islamic banking perspective, OCC interpretive activity *is* ijtihad. It thus demonstrates Islam's universality not just as a way of living a pious life but as a universally extendible knowledge-generating procedure.

This is a two-way street too. The OCC needs murabaha and other kinds of contractual forms to warrant the universality of its own practice. Without new contractual forms to interpret and provide rulings on, the OCC has no purpose. The presence of phenomena like Islamic banking gives the OCC its raison d'être. In this case, Islamic banking and the OCC each provides the formatting for the other without which the other cannot be imagined and cannot function, whether as an apparatus making things happen in the world or a technique making things in the world visible.

It is important to stress the ijtihad in Islam and in a regulatory environment that emphasizes interpretation over new legislation or statutes because in neither case is the book closed, as it were, on the permissibility of or even the need for Islamic mortgage alternatives. Shaykh Yusuf Abdullah al-Qaradawi ruled for the European Council for Fatwa and Research that Muslims living in the West are permitted to purchase homes using conventional, interest-based mortgages provided that: the borrower is purchasing the house for himself or herself and his or her household; the borrower does not have another house; and the borrower has no other assets that would permit him or her to purchase a house without the mortgage.[15] Al-Qaradawi based this ruling on the principle of darurah, or necessity when there is no other alternative, and the Qur'anic verse "Allah has made for you in your home an abode" (Qur'an, An-Nahl 80). Many of the people I interviewed who were clients or potential clients of American Islamic home financing companies knew of this ruling. For some, it relieved their anxieties about purchasing a home using a conventional, interest-based mortgage.[16]

American media reports about Islamic banking, however, almost always stress the unequivocal banning of interest in Islam, translating riba freely as "interest" or "usury" and often quoting American Muslims who rent rather than pay interest. Often these articles stress the lack of "choice" Islam affords observant Muslims. In an interview for *Religion and Ethics Newsweekly,* Islamic economics professor Mahmoud El-Gamal pointed out that only some Muslims consider the ban on interest to apply to them:

> There is a group of Muslims who view the prohibition of riba as historically predicated on the circumstances in Arabia at the time, which is that lending with interest is mostly an activity of loan sharks who used it to exploit the needy. They don't see the mortgage loan contract to be exploitative in any way and therefore don't feel that that is the forbidden riba. But even those people who feel that way have lingering doubts in their minds so that if Islamic financing could be provided competitively, I think many people would migrate over just for the peace of mind.[17]

The next chapter examines two distinct models of Islamic home financing in some detail. Here I merely wish to point out that the entire endeavor of seeing a need for, creating, and purchasing Islamic mortgages depends on several interpretive acts that are understood as such acts by participants in the Islamic home finance scene.

Islamic banking professionals debate endlessly whether a contract that looks and behaves so much like a conventional mortgage contract as to be indistinguishable from it from the point of view of conventional banking and finance regulations is in fact "Islamic." The OCC, for example, treats the markup paid in a murabaha contract and the rent paid in an ijara contract as interest for the purposes of tax reporting. SHAPE's online MALT™ calculator looks and works exactly like any other mortgage calculator. Those Islamic mortgage companies that have established relationships with Freddie Mac use Freddie Mac's standard mortgage forms and paperwork, with addenda detailing that the word "interest" is to be replaced with the words "rent" or "profit." Thus, many observers wonder whether Islamic mortgage contracts merely substitute the *word* "interest" with "markup," "profit," "administrative fees," or "rent," but not the *reality.* What if the markup is quoted as a percentage rate, as it is with the Guidance Financial model and MALT™? Guidance Financial offers the potential home buyer these words of solace: "*Halal* potato chips may be offered at the same price as a famous brand of potato chips that contain lard. The pricing of the potato chips, though the same, does not alter the nature of the product" (Guidance Financial 2004, 4, italics in original).

In a posting to the Islamic Banking and Finance Internet listserv that has been operating since 1998 and is one of the main international forums for discussion and debate among Islamic banking professionals, Mahmoud El-Gamal quoted the famous Islamic jurist M. Taqi Usmani as saying that "what we are developing now is not fiqh-ul-mu'amalat (jurisprudence of financial transactions), but rather fiqh-ul-Hiyal (jurisprudence of legal stratagems)—to circumvent the Shari'a."[18] El-Gamal intended to be critical of the kind of legal hairsplitting in which Islamic banking and finance professionals sometimes engage as they develop contractual forms with an Islamic veneer that they use mainly for the purpose of marketing.[19]

In the debate over Islamic mortgages in the United Kingdom, Haitham al-Haddad (2004, 5) issued a fatwa on December 12, 2004, arguing that HSBC's Amanah Finance and two other companies' mortgage replacement products ought to be considered "totally prohibited," since there was "no significant difference" between them and conventional riba mortgages. He based his argument on the "ambiguity" of the contract: "Is it a lease contract, a purchase contract or a combination of the two?" The ambiguity itself makes the mortgage replacement product unpermissible. Furthermore, if it is a form of "combined contract"—that is, two contracts in one—then it is probably prohibited, since "the Prophet (peace and blessings of Allah be upon him) prohibited two transactions in one" (1). Finally, the mortgage replacement product contains enough characteristics of a conventional loan to make it suspect—for example, the down payment and the payment of home insurance by the borrower, not the lender. If the client is thus considered the owner, responsible for insurance, maintenance, and other costs of homeownership as well as securing title with a down payment, then "this contract is *not* a lease contract in the first place" (2). While each of the subcontracts making up the lease-to-purchase model may, on its own, be completely halal (Islamically acceptable), if, in their totality, they have the effect of replicating riba, then the whole product is haram (Islamically forbidden).

In a response to this fatwa posted on the IBFNet Internet listserv, Hood Bradford of the Islamic University of Medinah challenged Haddad's ruling by asserting the provisional nature of ijtihad. In the "science of Fiqh," he wrote, discussions over "a lease which ends in ownership" have been "differed over by all the major scholars. Why? Because it is an area of Ijtihad. There are no clear cut right and wrong answers in ijtihad as you will all know, and one can never criticize the ijtihad of a certain scholar over another scholar's ijtihad when the whole issue is one of ijtihad!"[20]

What is an Islamic mortgage? On the one hand, it is a lease-to-own contract, or a cost-plus markup contract, or a profit-and-loss-sharing contract used for the purpose of financing the purchase of a home without resorting to interest. It might be some combination of these arrangements. On the other hand, it depends . . . on interpretation, and on who is doing the interpreting.

CHAPTER THREE

POSTMODERN AND PURITAN:
A TALE OF TWO COMPANIES

Most of my quantitative and ethnographic research involved only two of the handful of companies that offer Islamic mortgage replacement products. As noted in the last chapter, many such companies are relatively new to the scene; indeed, most came into existence as I was in the middle of conducting this research. The two companies whose products and practices I examine more fully are well known both in Islamic banking circles and among many American Muslims. I discussed in the introduction my reasons for replacing their real names with pseudonyms in this chapter and the two that follow. Doing so does not completely disguise their identities, of course. I ask readers already familiar with Islamic mortgages in the United States to suspend disbelief and approach the material presented in these chapters as if from a distance so that the whole can be more easily grasped, fully recognizing that this apprehension of the whole is purely the effect of a trick of scale.

TWO MODELS

"Ijara" is an Islamic finance company that offers a mortgage replacement product that can be used for a home purchase as well as a refinancing loan. That product resembles the medieval vif-gage in some key respects. Ijara prides itself on a carefully articulated product modeled on an ijara contract from classical Islamic jurisprudence. Its product also has a clear exegetical basis; that is, it has a clear basis in Islamic traditions of jurisprudence and interpretation. An ijara contract is essentially a lease-to-own contract. The client and company enter into a partnership agreement whereby the client agrees to pay back a predetermined amount of the principal every month, plus a proportion of the property's fair market rental value. That proportion is determined by the client's share of the ownership of the property. Over time the rent paid decreases as the client's ownership share increases. The rental value is "marked to market" at the time the contract is drawn up. That is, the company determines the rental value of the property based on prevailing local market conditions. If the property is a two-bedroom, one-bath, twelve-hundred-square-foot house, Ijara looks at the rental value for comparable properties in the area in order to set the rent.

If an applicant named Bilal wants a mortgage with Ijara for a house worth $100,000 and has the money for a 20 percent down payment (Ijara's standard until recently, accounting perhaps for its higher-than-expected number of wealthier applicants, as described in the next chapter), he becomes a 20 percent co-owner of the property and Ijara becomes an 80 percent co-owner. In the first month Bilal pays back a predetermined amount of the "principal" together with 80 percent of the monthly fair market rental value of the property. In effect, he pays the remaining 20 percent of the rent to himself. The next month his share ownership of the house has increased, and so the proportion of the monthly rent due to Ijara decreases (see figure 3.1).

I chose the name Bilal in this hypothetical example because Ijara's model draws inspiration from the following hadith:

> Abu Sa'id reported: Bilal (Allah be pleased with him) came with [dates of] fine quality. . . . Allah's Messenger (may peace be upon him) said to him: "From where you have brought them?" Bilal said: "We had inferior quality . . . dates and I exchanged two *sa*'s of inferior quality with one *sa* of fine quality as food for Allah's Apostle (may peace be upon him)," whereupon Allah's Messenger (may peace be upon him) said: "Woe! It is in fact usury; therefore, don't do that. But when you intend to buy dates of superior quality, sell [those of] the inferior quality in a separate bargain and then [buy those of] the superior quality."[1]

Ijara and other professionals and academics in the field of Islamic banking and finance use the Bilal hadith to argue that God prohibited riba to

FIGURE 3.1   Ijara's Ijara Model

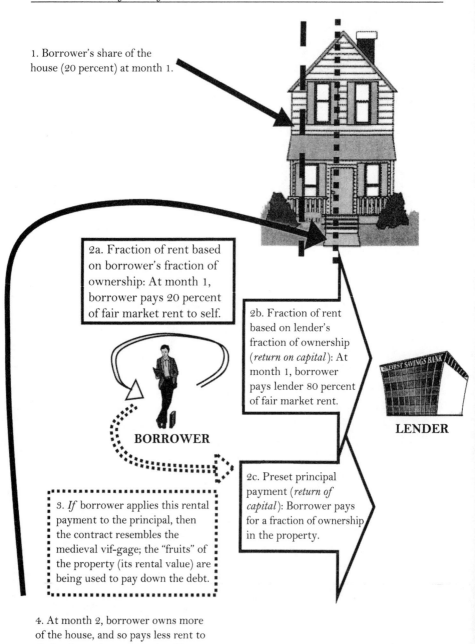

1. Borrower's share of the house (20 percent) at month 1.

2a. Fraction of rent based on borrower's fraction of ownership: At month 1, borrower pays 20 percent of fair market rent to self.

2b. Fraction of rent based on lender's fraction of ownership (*return on capital*): At month 1, borrower pays lender 80 percent of fair market rent.

BORROWER

LENDER

2c. Preset principal payment (*return of capital*): Borrower pays for a fraction of ownership in the property.

3. *If* borrower applies this rental payment to the principal, then the contract resembles the medieval vif-gage; the "fruits" of the property (its rental value) are being used to pay down the debt.

4. At month 2, borrower owns more of the house, and so pays less rent to the lender and more rent to self.

Source: Author's compilation.

prevent injustice by ensuring equality in market transactions. Barter and trade, of course, make equal transactions difficult, since they always involve comparisons of unlike goods and services. Money as a universal equivalent is supposed to mitigate the valuation anomalies introduced by barter. Hence, in the Bilal hadith, adhering to the prohibition of riba requires that the ratio of barter trade equal the ratio of market prices. As Mahmoud El-Gamal (2000a) argues, we have in this hadith a specification for the conditions for Pareto efficiency in the market. Bilal should have marked his poor dates to the market by selling them for the highest price he could get. Then he should have purchased high-quality dates with the money thus obtained at the lowest price he could find. In so doing, he would have brought traders' desires into alignment with market mechanisms. This is what the Prophet demanded of him. And this confirms the market itself, the mechanism for equating utilities with prices, as at one with divine plan.

Because it is a leasing contract, a standard ijara contract would, in the American regulatory environment, require that the lessee be the title-holder of the property. Ijara has circumvented this problem by granting title to the client but holding a lien against it. This means that Ijara's model consists of several distinct contracts: lien; the creation of a joint partnership between Ijara and the client that determines the disposition of the shares in the *property* (not, importantly, some other entity, like a corporate partnership); and then, subsequently, the transfer of shares of the property to the client over time. Monthly payments consist of a return-of-capital portion and a return-on-capital portion. The former is the purchase of the company's shares; the latter is the payment to the company of its proportion of the rent. The return-on-capital portion is determined by marking the property to market, not by an interest rate. Hence, the significance of the Bilal hadith and the exegetical warrant underlying Ijara's model.

Since the client and the company have agreed from the start that the client—and only the client—will repurchase shares in the property from the company and will do so immediately upon payment for those shares with each monthly payment, the company can have the title held in the name of the client. Other lease-to-purchase mortgage models sometimes consist of two distinct contracts: the leasing contract, by which the company and the client agree to the rental rate that the client is to pay on top of the principal; and the sale contract, which binds the client to the eventual purchase of the house and the company to its eventual sale to the client and to no one else (see Morris and Thomas 2002, 20–21). When it began its ijara-based mortgage replacement business, Ijara referred to its contract as a simple ijara contract. As it dealt with the legal restrictions that require the lessee to maintain the title to the property as well as be responsible for the expenses of owning the house (such as real estate taxes and insurance, which can be passed off to the client in the form of an increased rent if it is agreed to by both parties at the initiation of the contract) and came up with the model whereby the client purchases shares in the property immediately upon payment and also holds title, Ijara labeled its contract an "ijara/diminishing musharaka" contract. The "diminishing musharaka" element refers to the corporate partnership that is established between the client and the company to manage the disposition of the shares in the property that are being transferred with each monthly payment. The term of an Ijara mortgage replacement product can be fifteen or thirty years. The paperwork is the standard Freddie Mac mortgage application plus a patented financing agreement that describes the relationship between the company and the client. Rent payments can be deducted as home mortgage interest on the client's federal income tax returns. (Although the Internal Revenue Service has not formally ruled on the permissibility of this, it has accepted the deduction.)

Ijara's model works like the medieval vif-gage, with a couple of important differences (see table 3.1). As in a vif-gage, the property is "alive" to both the company and the client in that its "yield"—its value as a rental property—is paid to both partners in the transaction each month. More specifically, it is a vif-gage from the point of view of the client, who has two roles: as the functional equivalent of a mortgagor in a conventional mortgage, and as an owner. As an owner, the client receives a portion of the fruits of the property each month in the form of rent: as the client's ownership share increases, so does his or her share of that rent. If the client uses that rent to pay down the principal, then the living product of the property is, in effect, paying down the loan and the contract is a vif-gage, not a mort-gage. But this would depend on how the client manages his or her rental income and is not a given in the structure of the contract, only a possibility. From the point of view of the company, however, the Ijara mortgage replacement product is more like a medieval mort-gage, since the rent received by Ijara is not applied to the principal of the loan and instead is considered Ijara's profit. A medieval English jurist might very well have interpreted this rent as usurious—like riba, usury for our imaginary English jurist referred not just to interest on a loan but also to unlawful gain. If that profit was understood to be compensation for undertaking the risk of the investment with the client, or if that profit was understood to fluctuate as rental market values fluctuated, then our medieval jurist would probably not have viewed the profit as usurious. Again, however, the resolution and avoidance of usury is not a given in the struc-

TABLE 3.1   Ijara's Mortgage Replacement Versus Medieval Gages

	Ijara	Vif-Gage	Mortgage
Status of property to lender (for gages) or company or co-owner (for Ijara)	Alive	Alive	Dead
Status of property to borrower (for gages) or client or co-owner (for Ijara)	Alive	Alive	Dead, especially if borrower defaults
Yield pays down the debt?	Yes, if the client or co-owner uses client's share of the rent to make principal payments No, from the point of view of the company or co-owner	Yes	No

Source: Author's compilation.

ture of the product—from the point of view of medieval English law—but only a possibility, contingent on the company's good faith and intentions.

Ijara bases its model on its founders' interpretation of various fatwas proclaimed by internationally respected jurists such as Shaykh Yusuf Abdullah al-Qaradawi. It also takes a critical stance on the credentials and overlapping (perhaps conflicting) interests of members of other Islamic finance corporations' shari'a supervisory boards. One of the main targets of its attacks, implicitly if not explicitly, is its main competitor, "Searchlight."

Searchlight's model is different from Ijara's. Based on a musharaka contract from Islamic jurisprudence, Searchlight's mortgage replacement product looks like a conventional mortgage because it appears to include a rate-based interest payment. The tax implications are the same, and the payments may work out to be similar. It functions rather differently, however. A musharaka contract is a co-ownership contract without any specification as to whether or how ownership might change over time. Searchlight and the client enter into a corporate partnership and form a limited liability company (LLC) together. The object of the contract they create is the LLC, not the property the client seeks to purchase. The LLC owns the property, and the company and the client recalculate their percentage share in the partnership—not in the property—over the term of the contract (fifteen, twenty, or thirty years). Searchlight also invites other potential investors to share in the ownership of the LLC. (See figures 3.1 and 3.2 for a comparison of the Ijara and Searchlight models.)

Using LLCs allows Searchlight to provide a mechanism for other investors or agencies (Freddie Mac, for example) to add capital to the Islamic mortgage market. Freddie Mac can first purchase a share in several LLCs held jointly between Searchlight and its clients, and then it can create securities in its co-owned assets for trade on the secondary market. (The secondary market in Islamic mortgages, which now involves Searchlight, Ijara, and other Islamic mortgage companies in the United States, is discussed in chapter 6.) As with Ijara, Searchlight's relationship with Freddie Mac has required the use of standardized mortgage application and disclosure forms; these forms include terms like "loan," "interest," "lender," and "borrower." Searchlight's shari'a supervisory board has determined that such usages do not invalidate the essential nature of the diminishing musharaka contract at the heart of Searchlight's mortgage alternative model.

Searchlight's model consists of a musharaka partnership grafted onto a "declining balance" component, whereby one owner (the client) gradually buys out the other owner (the company). This makes it look similar to an ijara contract, but with one exception: whereas in ijara a monthly rent is assessed based on market values and this rent determines the monthly markup (which takes the place of an interest payment in a conventional non-Islamic loan), in Searchlight's "diminishing co-ownership" model the monthly markup is an "administrative fee" added to Searchlight's "profit" from the co-ownership arrangement and that fee is arbitrarily set by Searchlight. It may resemble rent, and it may be described as rent, but it is not necessarily set by rental market values and is not technically speaking a payment for the enjoyment of the property. Searchlight calls this portion of the monthly payment the "profit payment." The portion of the monthly payment for the client's additional shares in the LLC it terms the "acquisition payment." As with Ijara's product, the occupant or client is responsible for all property taxes and maintenance costs, since payment of these costs is considered to benefit the occupant, who maintains sole enjoyment of the property.

Searchlight explicitly states that it seeks a profit payment that is competitive with the interest rates available in the broader home finance market. It also states that its profit payments may be linked to an interest rate index (such as LIBOR, the London Interbank Lending Rate). Searchlight uses the same Bilal hadith as Ijara to justify this practice but

FIGURE 3.2   Searchlight's Diminishing Musharaka Model

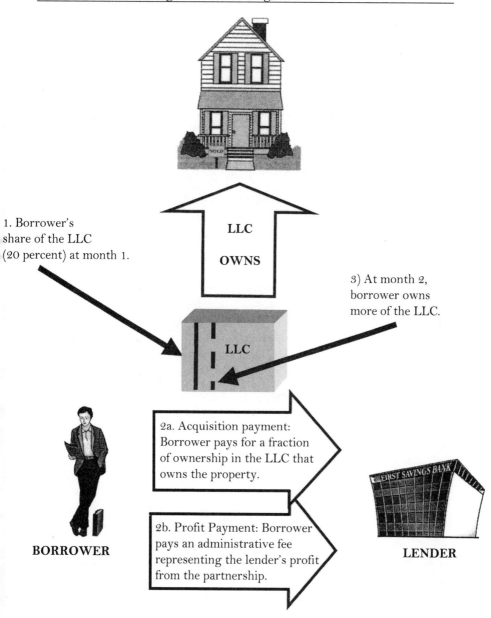

1. Borrower's share of the LLC (20 percent) at month 1.

LLC OWNS

3) At month 2, borrower owns more of the LLC.

LLC

2a. Acquisition payment: Borrower pays for a fraction of ownership in the LLC that owns the property.

2b. Profit Payment: Borrower pays an administrative fee representing the lender's profit from the partnership.

BORROWER

LENDER

Source: Author's compilation.

interprets it differently. Rather than seeing an exhortation to mark to market, Searchlight interprets the Bilal hadith as stating that a transaction is permissible even if the benefit it confers is similar to that of a prohibited transaction.

According to Searchlight, the profit payment is not technically "interest" since it is not based on the capital Searchlight extends to the client but rather on the business partnership that the company establishes with its client. The reasoning goes something like this: As a business partner in a joint enterprise with the client, Searchlight expects a profit for its services. The chief service it provides, in addition to its administrative expertise, is to permit its partner the sole use and enjoyment of the house that their partnership owns. It reaps this profit in the form of a markup paid by the client. The net result may look quite similar to interest charges. As Searchlight's promotional material explains, however, "we do not change the math; we change the way we do business." As with Ijara's rent payments, Searchlight's profit payments can be claimed as interest deductions on the client's federal income tax returns.

Searchlight boasts a shari'a supervisory board made up of internationally recognized scholars and jurists. It launched an aggressive marketing campaign in 2002 and continues to have high visibility nationally through its presence at Islamic conferences, in mosques, and in articles placed in American Muslim newspapers and magazines.

POSTMODERN OR PURITAN?

There has been a large and lengthy debate in Islamic banking and finance about the relative status of contracts like musharaka compared to ijara and mudaraba (profit-and-loss-sharing). Scholars and practitioners often deride the former because they insulate the company from the risks of doing business. Ijara contracts are deemed more "pure" because they have a clearer exegetical basis, and mudaraba is deemed more equitable because it spreads the risk by sharing losses between company and client. Musharaka and its close cousin murabaha (a cost-plus contract) are seen as more "efficient," but their theological status is in some doubt (see El-Gamal 2000b; Saleh 1986). Islamic banking and finance scholars and professionals have agonized over the merits of these contractual forms; while many tend to feel better about leasing and profit-and-loss sharing than they do about cost-plus or profit-based contracts, many also recognize that the latter are simpler, more efficient, and more profitable in the long run. Because of this debate, and because Searchlight's profit payment is tied to an interest rate, I assumed at the start of my research that Ijara would attract more conservative Muslims who sought to adhere as closely as possible to the Qur'anic prohibition of riba, while Searchlight would attract those willing to experiment or those content with a shari'a stamp of approval from known public figures even if the product "looked like" an interest-based mortgage from an end-user's perspective.

However, the people I interviewed who had detailed or even cursory knowledge of Ijara and Searchlight tended to claim that "Ijara is not really shari'a," or that Ijara "is not as shari'a as Searchlight," as two interviewees put it. The latter comment is interesting because it understands differences in shari'a compliance quantitatively rather than qualitatively. People think Ijara is "less" shari'a-compliant than Searchlight. Legal debates within Islamic banking for at least the past twenty years might suggest otherwise. So too might the end-user client, who sees on his or her yearly statement what looks like an amortization chart with columns indicating acquisition payments and profit payments that mirror precisely—down to the numbers and percentages—principal payments and interest payments.

When I began this research, I had expected Searchlight to be more pluralistic in its conception of Islamic law because its staff members had told me that its potential client base was more open to various interpretations, less rigid in their thinking, and even "postmodern." One employee spoke of plans to set up operations in California specifically to capitalize on California Muslims' supposedly greater "flexibility" in matters of religion. In contrast, Ijara employees spoke of appealing to "puritans" who were concerned with the "fundamentals of Islam." Throughout the course of my research, however, almost everyone who had some knowledge of Searchlight's product spoke of it as having greater religious or "shari'a" weight than Ijara's.

The quantitative data presented in the next chapter add a layer of complexity to this apparent paradox, for it appears that more conservative Muslims are drawn to Searchlight's product, not Ijara's. In chapter 8, I argue that the paradox can be explained in terms of the changing status of Islamic legal traditions and practices in the United States. Khaled Abou El Fadl (1998, 41) has noted that "in the United States the field of shari'a is flooded with self-declared experts who inundate our discourses with self-indulgent babble and gibberish." Karen Leonard (2003) has outlined the various efforts to create national-level fiqh councils in the United States, particularly the efforts of the Islamic Society of North America and the Islamic Circle of North America (see also DeLorenzo

1998). Some members of the resultant Fiqh Council of North America sit on the shari'a supervisory board of Searchlight. Leonard (2003, 63) cites Abou El Fadl's characterization of the current situation of Islamic knowledge in the United States as having "produced a landscape devoid of respect for the schools and methods of Islamic legal scholarship and for pluralism." She reports on Ihsan Bagby, Paul Perl, and Bryan Froehle's (2001) survey research indicating that imams and presidents of mosques in the United States cite the Qur'an (95 percent) and Sunnah (90 percent) as "absolutely foundational," while the various schools of Islamic law are seen as of "little or no importance" (52 percent) or only "somewhat important" (25 percent). Where do Searchlight and Ijara fit in this picture, and how can we square Searchlight's model with people's assertions that it is "more shari'a" with its "postmodern" aspirations? Likewise, how can we square Ijara's model with people's assertions that it is "less shari'a" with its "puritan" aspirations?

Searchlight has a strong and persuasive marketing operation, as well as an Internet presence that looks high-tech, savvy, and professional. Its animated logo consists of the two words "Modern Values" juxtaposed together, then separating as the words "Finance" and "Timeless" interject themselves to produce "Modern Finance, Timeless Values." It has a shari'a supervisory board made up of truly prominent individuals who have issued fatwas on Searchlight's products, which are then posted on the company web page for all to read (and to see the signatures of the jurists warranting the products). It is interesting, however, that the content of these fatwas seems less important than their form. They actually say very little; one such statement, for example, reads: "After reviewing the mechanism as well as the agreements and documents, and after suggesting amendments that have been incorporated, the Shari'a Supervisory Board is of the view that given the circumstances prevailing in the United States, this arrangement conforms to the rules and principles of the Shari'a; and therefore, Muslims may avail themselves of this opportunity to acquire homes and properties by means of this method." There is no citing of authority or text or school of law in this statement. There is only the affirmation that the shari'a supervisory board warrants the model.

For its part, Ijara (which has never had as snazzy a corporate marketing strategy but has relied more on the charisma and leadership of its founder) has gone on the attack, offering advice on how to select a home finance company that includes the following admonitions: "Please: Do not get overly impressed by intensive advertising that features 'Shari'aa [*sic*] Boards' with religious rulings [or] 'fatwa'!" It also advises clients to ask their finance professionals, "Is it a Model that uses interest as a foundation for its calculations? If they immediately quote you a rate, this is nothing but interest." Furthermore, "Does the institution use intensive marketing concepts using religious slogans to 'sell' its services and operations?" "Does the company re-invest in the community?"

Often in the course of this research almost all of my interviewees who were not employees of either company asked me to adjudicate the status of Ijara's versus Searchlight's products. I resisted the call, although I sometimes got into animated and entertaining exchanges with people about how the different products work. "But it's tied to an interest rate!" several exclaimed, referring to Searchlight's model; nevertheless, they often ended up admitting a preference for that model over Ijara's because of its backing by prominent scholars. As I discuss in chapter 5, many even mistakenly believed that Searchlight's product was based on an ijara contract. Ijara's product seemed "more correct" only if what counted as shari'a compliance was a literal interpretation of religious texts, and only if the work of Islamic banking was understood to proceed from those texts rather than to constitute, in itself, its own kind of religious or exegetical activity. This is a key point. My sense is that those who are intellectually captivated by Ijara's model prefer it over Searchlight's. Indeed, Ijara makes an effort to engage the potential client (or interested researcher) in the exegetical act and the work of interpretation itself. It is fun and intellectually interesting to work out the legal and religious warrants of an ijara contract, to read hadith on leasing, and to ruminate on the market mechanism as a manifestation of the divine. Searchlight does not offer the same kind of hands-on and personal relationship with its model. The model simply exists and is offered to potential clients as a predetermined, authorized contractual form. Its warrants are the fatwas. Form trumps content, and the mere fact of the existence of the fatwas underwrites the entire enterprise.

If Ijara represents shari'a as a textualist endeavor backed by the intellectual activities of human beings talking and debating with one another as they assess a property's rental value, and its living yield as a tangible asset, Searchlight represents shari'a as a practical activity best understood as the working-out of their model and its form itself under the guidance of the esteemed fiqh scholars and experts who sit on its shari'a supervisory board. "We do not change the math," Searchlight proclaims. The form is the same, and it is not the content that is different from a conventional mortgage so much as the form's own activity as it moves from fatwa to monthly payment.

CHAPTER FOUR

WHO WANTS ISLAMIC MORTGAGE ALTERNATIVES?

What are the demographic characteristics of people who want an Islamic mortgage? And who chooses which Islamic mortgage alternative? Are more conservative Muslims with strict, literalist interpretations of Islamic law drawn to Ijara's product, which is based on rent rather than a profit payment that resembles an interest rate? Are more progressive Muslims willing to embrace Searchlight's less complicated product? The analysis of available quantitative data suggests exactly the opposite.

In 2002 Home Mortgage Disclosure Act (HMDA) data became available for the first time for Islamic home finance companies. Implemented by Regulation C of the Federal Reserve Board and enacted in 1975, HMDA requires that loan data be made publicly available in order to determine whether lenders and other financial institutions are meeting the housing needs of their communities, to identify discriminatory lending practices or patterns, and to provide information to public officials charged with attracting private-sector investment. HMDA data are disseminated by the Federal Financial Institutions Examination Council (FFIEC) and are available in raw form online at www.ffiec.gov. Currently, depository institutions with assets of $32 million or less and non-depository institutions with assets of $10 million or less and fewer than 100 home purchase loan originations (including refinancings) are exempt from HMDA data collection. Until 2002, Islamic home financing compa-

56

nies had not crossed the exemption threshold. Data from 2002 and 2003 were available at the time of this writing.

HMDA data are usually used for fair lending monitoring and enforcement. They are also notoriously unreliable. The data are collected from mortgage or refinancing paperwork on which borrowers or sometimes lending agents report the sex and race of the borrower. This information is compiled with data on income level, which are reported in terms of deviation from the median of a borrower's census tract, or metropolitan statistical area (MSA). Race data are particularly problematic and often missing, especially when lenders collect information by mail or phone (Huck 2001). Elvin Wyly and Steve Holloway (2002) note that the second-largest racial-ethnic category reported in HMDA data is "information not provided." Many housing policy researchers make their careers by finding statistical or other solutions to the shortcomings of HMDA data; their results are controversial, however, because they do not always shed light on the problems the data are supposed to help identify (see, for example, Munnell et al. 1996; Ross and Yinger 2002; Squires and O'Connor 2001).

For the following analyses, I created a dataset from the 2,507 applications to both companies in 2002 and 2003 from HMDA data. The dataset includes all applications for conventional loans and refinancing loans and specifies whether they were accepted, denied, or withdrawn. HMDA refers to primary mortgages as "conventional loans" and to second mortgages or refinancings as "refinancing loans." (Although it may cause some confusion, since Islamic banking professionals refer to non-Islamic, interest-based mortgages as "conventional loans," I maintain HMDA terminology in this chapter and refer to loans for primary mortgages as conventional loans.) The refinancing loans here are all cases in which a borrower used a refinancing loan to convert his or her non-Islamic, interest-based mortgage to an Islamic mortgage.

The numbers of loan and refinancing applications might seem small, but the public presence of Ijara and Searchlight is quite large. Ijara has sponsored international conferences on Islamic banking and finance for the past ten years and grants yearly awards for contributions to the field of Islamic economics and finance. Searchlight has embarked on a major advertising campaign that includes the sponsorship of important national events (Islamic Society of North America conferences, for example), and some of its shari'a supervisors have become spokespeople for Muslim issues and interests in the United States. These supervisors have taken the mantle of "Islamic law" out of the fiqh councils and into the communities they serve, and as I argue in chapter 8, they are transforming Islamic law in the process.

Data for Ijara and Searchlight seem to be of better quality than HMDA data for other lenders, although here as well there is a substantial degree of nonreporting of race, as well as some other glitches (for example, missing or incomplete data for some MSAs). From the point of view of fair lending concerns, which usually have to do with differential denial rates, it is striking that Ijara and Searchlight have not had much of a denial rate at all. In 2002 Searchlight did not reject any applications for either conventional loans or refinancing loans out of a total of 29 and 116, respectively. Ijara rejected one conventional loan application out of a total of 251, and four applications were withdrawn, for a total denial rate of 2 percent. It rejected no refinancing applications out of a total of 77. In 2003 there were more denials overall, but not significantly so compared with national averages. Searchlight rejected 17 out of 475 refinancing applications (4 percent) and 89 out of 890 conventional loan applications (1 percent). Ijara rejected 3 out of 201 refinancing applications (1 percent) and 13 out of 253 conventional loan applications (5 percent). The denial rate nationally for all lenders is about 18 percent.[1]

In this chapter, I use the terms "conservative" and "progressive" to refer to some mortgage applicants, but I am not comfortable with these terms, and in chapter 5 I explain why these terms are inadequate to describe the complexity of Islamic legal norms in the United States. When I first presented an overview of the patterns in the quantitative data discussed in this chapter to a non-Muslim colleague, she assumed that by "conservative" Muslim I meant women who dress modestly, cover, and "keep silent" and men who "make their wives walk three paces behind and don't listen to what they have to say." In using the term "conservative," I am aware that I may call up this stereotype in the minds of some readers. In addition, the proxy measure for conservatism here—whether a person is listed as a "male" instead of a "joint" applicant despite marital status—may have more to say about belief (or aspiration) than actual practice. A man who wishes to be, or thinks he is, in charge of a household's finances may, of course, be living a fantasy. Furthermore, a strict interpretation of the sources of Islamic law may ultimately warrant what many in the United States would consider a progressive politics, a commitment to social justice, and a strong belief in gender equality. This kind of strict interpretation of Islamic law, when wedded to American minority struggles for political recognition, may even further confound the stereotypical assessment of "conservative" Islam. As one young woman explained her antiracist political orientation to me, "I am Muslim, I am a woman, I wear hijab, but I am a woman of color."

WHO "BORROWS" FROM ISLAMIC "LENDERS"?

Both Ijara and Searchlight have a wide geographic distribution of lending activity. Ijara, an older company with licenses to operate in all states except New York (as of 2005), has a broader national scope than Searchlight. Searchlight, in business only since 2001, operates in eleven states and the District of Columbia.[2] In 2002, although there was overlap in their regions of operation, the companies seemed to be in direct competition in only two MSAs: the Chicago area and the Baltimore area. In 2003 the two companies were in direct competition in the cities of Ann Arbor, Baltimore, Chicago, and Detroit, the states of California, Florida, and New Jersey, and the Washington, D.C., metropolitan area. Table 4.1 lists the states from which applications originated in 2002 and 2003. One striking thing about the geographic data is the extent to which Ijara has a presence even in smaller, southern, and central states compared to Searchlight, whose activity is concentrated in states with large urban centers. Because Ijara has a longer history and has relied on word of mouth and the Internet, while Searchlight advertises mainly through Muslim organizations, Ijara has been more successful in reaching isolated Muslims who may not have a large community around them. The geographic data suggest that Searchlight, which has conducted a tightly focused marketing campaign since its founding, concentrates on reaching areas with potentially large Muslim communities and thus a potentially large market. Ijara, by contrast, has concerned itself since its founding with reaching out to Muslims anywhere who seek an interest-free alternative.

The two companies have virtually opposite profiles in terms of the types of loan applications they receive. For both years combined, Ijara received more than one and a half times as many conventional loan applications as refinancing applications; Searchlight received twice as many refinancing applications as conventional loan applications. Searchlight comes closer to the national statistics: in 2002 and 2003, 26.5 percent of all loan applications nationally were for conventional mortgages while 73.5 percent were for refinancing loans. This reflects the period of historically low interest rates. Searchlight's initial business model and marketing campaign focused on encouraging Muslim homeowners to refinance their existing interest-based mortgage with an Islamic mortgage; it has continued to emphasize refinancing over new home purchases. Ijara has

TABLE 4.1   Islamic Loan Activity by State, 2002 and 2003

	Ijara		Searchlight	
	2002	2003	2002	2003
Alabama	0%	0.1%	0%	0%
Arizona	0	1	0	0
Arkansas	0	0.6	0	0
California	12	12	0	7
Colorado	1	0.8	0	0
Connecticut	0.6	2	0	0
D.C.	0	2	62	19
Florida	5	6	0	11
Georgia	4	7	0	0
Illinois	13	4	8	26
Indiana	1	1	0	0
Iowa	0.6	0.4	0	0
Kansas	0	0.3	0	0
Kentucky	0.3	0.3	0	0
Louisiana	0	0.4	0	0
Maryland	3	1	10	4
Massachusetts	1	4	0	0
Michigan	16	9	0	7
Minnesota	8	2	0	0
Missouri	0.3	2	0	0
Nebraska	0	0.1	0	0
Nevada	0.3	0	0	0
New Jersey	1	7	19	14
New York	0	0	0	3
North Carolina	1	3	0	0
Ohio	1	1	0	1
Oklahoma	1	0.6	0	0
Oregon	0.3	1	0	0
Pennsylvania	0	0.1	0	4
South Carolina	0	0.8	0	0
Tennessee	0	3	0	0
Texas	23	18	0	0
Virginia	0	0.1	0.6	0.6
Washington	1	3	0	0
Data not available	3	6	0	3

Source: Author's compilation.
Note: According to HMDA data, no Islamic mortgages were taken out in 2002 or 2003 in the following states: Alaska, Delaware, Hawaii, Idaho, Maine, Mississippi, Montana, New Hampshire, New Mexico, North Dakota, Rhode Island, South Dakota, Utah, Vermont, West Virginia, Wisconsin, Wyoming.

focused on first-time home buyers but in 2003 began to branch out into the refinancing market. Reflected here are both Ijara's mission to reach Muslims who may have stayed out of the housing market altogether because of their views on Islam's prohibition of interest and Searchlight's strategy of reaching Muslims who already have an interest-based mortgage and are looking for a more shari'a-compliant alternative (see table 4.2). Based on this lending profile, we might assume that Ijara's clients are more conservative, since they have stayed out of the mortgage market altogether, while Searchlight's are less strict about avoiding interest since they have had an interest-based mortgage product in the past. This assumption, however, turns out to be incorrect.[3]

The gender and income profiles of applicants to each company differ as well. As can be seen in table 4.3, Ijara's applicants tend to file their mortgage paperwork jointly—that is, each spouse signs the paperwork and is legally responsible for the contract. Searchlight's applicants are

TABLE 4.2   Loan Type by Lender, 2002 and 2003

Year and Loan Type	Number of Loans (Percentage Within Lender)		
	All U.S. Lenders	Ijara	Searchlight
2002			
Conventional loans	4,522,973 (30.1%)	162 (73.6%)	25 (20.2%)
Refinancing loans	10,480,495 (69.9)	58 (26.4)	99 (79.8)
Total	15,003,468	220	124
2003			
Conventional loans	5,503,469 (24.1)	415 (61.6)	500 (33.6)
Refinancing loans	17,286,896 (75.9)	259 (38.4)	989 (66.4)
Total	22,790,365	674	1,489
2002 and 2003			
Conventional loans	10,026,442 (26.5)	577 (64.5)	525 (32.5)
Refinancing loans	27,767,391 (73.5)	317 (35.5)	1,088 (67.5)
Total	37,793,833	894	1,613

Source: Author's compilation.

TABLE 4.3   Lender by Gender, 2002 and 2003

Lender	Gender (Percentage Within Lender)			
	Female	Male	Joint	Total
Ijara	34 (3.8%)	347 (38.8%)	513 (57.4%)	894
Searchlight	120 (7.4)	1,202 (74.5)	291 (18.0)	1,613
Total Ijara and Searchlight	154 (6.1)	1,549 (61.8)	804 (32.1)	2,507
All U.S. lenders	7,738,284 (20.5)	9,861,181 (26.1)	20,194,368 (53.4)	37,793,833

Source: Author's compilation.

overwhelmingly more male. The differences are statistically significant, and various measures for testing the strength of the association
between categorical variables suggest a weak to decent relationship.[4]
What can we make of this difference? From a legal point of view, the
signature on the loan application does not determine who owns the
property. People may have many reasons for filling in one or both persons' names. And no matter what the paperwork says, people may have
different understandings of the disposition of ownership. In California,
a community property state, married couples enjoy joint rights to property. In addition, it is important to note that the "male" and "female" applicants may consist of either single adults applying for a loan or mortgage (who, with only one income, are more likely to be in the lower
income ranges in their metropolitan statistical area) or married couples
in which only the husband or only the wife (and probably the former)
fills out the loan paperwork. Fair lending advocates have found a sort of
"marriage effect": as income rises, fewer women apply for loans singly
(see, for example, New Jersey Citizen Action 1997) and more women
apply jointly with their husbands. In the case of Ijara and Searchlight,
however, the ethnographic data suggest that most loan applicants are
married. In the aggregated data for all U.S. lenders, the gender category on the application varies together with income level, owing perhaps to either the presence of two incomes in a household or a correla-
tion between more progressive views on the marriage relationship and
higher socioeconomic status.

The data on race are equally tricky (see table 4.4). A large proportion
of applications are marked "other" or "race not available." It is also diffi-

TABLE 4.4   Lender by Race, 2002 and 2003

Lender	Alaska Native or American Indian	Asian or Pacific Islander	Black	Hispanic	White	Mixed-Race Couple	Other or NA
Ijara	.1%	36.5%	4.0%	0%	26.1%	1.9%	31.4%
Searchlight	0	55.7	8.2	.5	14.3	1.5	19.8
Total	0	49.2	6.7	.3	18.4	1.6	23.8

Source: Author's compilation.

cult to interpret the HMDA racial categories. South Asian and Arab Americans might record themselves as "Asian or Pacific Islander," "other," or "white." Still, there are significant differences between the two companies and a weak relationship between race and choice of lender.[5] Based on interviews and ethnographic observations, Ijara attracts more white converts than Searchlight, whose client base is more South Asian. Many of my South Asian interviewees believed that Ijara attracts more Arabs than South Asians, although it is impossible to confirm this with HMDA data. If we assume that most people in the "Asian or Pacific Islander" category are South Asians, then it appears that the applicant pool for Islamic mortgages is overwhelmingly South Asian. There are few African American Muslims applying for Islamic mortgages. Leonard (2003, 4–5) summarizes various surveys of Muslim Americans by race; African Americans make up between 33 and 42 percent of all Muslim Americans in these surveys. It is interesting, then, that they are not being drawn into the Islamic mortgage market.

There are, of course, no HMDA data on sectarian allegiances such as Shi'a or Sunni. Leonard (2003, 34) reports that 15 to 20 percent of Muslim Americans are thought to be Shi'a. People who market Islamic mortgages say their primary market is Sunni Muslims but that Shi'a are drawn to them as well. There are no Shi'a scholars, however, on the shari'a supervisory boards of American Islamic mortgage companies.

Comparing Ijara's and Searchlight's applicant pools, there is a significant but very weak relationship between income level and choice of company.[6] HMDA data report income level in five ordinal categories based on the applicant's income as a percentage of the median income in his or her MSA. As seen in table 4.5, Searchlight's applicants tend to be poorer than Ijara's relative to those living around them in their MSA. This may in part be an effect of Searchlight's concentration in urban areas, where

TABLE 4.5 Lender by Income, 2002 and 2003

	Income Category by Percentage of Median Income (Percentage Within Lender)					
Lender	Less Than 50 Percent	50 to 79 Percent	80 to 99 Percent	100 to 119 Percent	120 Percent or More	Total
Ijara	59 (6.6%)	158 (17.7%)	140 (15.7%)	158 (17.7%)	379 (42.4%)	894
Searchlight	206 (12.8)	380 (23.6)	260 (16.1)	244 (15.1)	523 (32.4)	1,613
Total Ijara and Searchlight	265 (10.6)	538 (21.5)	400 (16.0)	402 (16.0)	902 (36.0)	2,507
All U.S. lenders	3,319,446 (8.8)	7,444,360 (19.7)	5,162,392 (13.7)	4,634,132 (12.3)	17,233,504 (45.6)	37,793,833

Source: Author's compilation.

incomes are higher, although data from individual MSAs from which both companies have received applications suggest that Searchlight's applicants overall are less wealthy than Ijara's. This may also reflect the fact that historically Ijara has required higher down payments (sometimes 20 percent) than Searchlight (usually 5 to 10 percent), although in the years for which data are reported Ijara increasingly accepted lower down payments in order to be competitive with Searchlight.

Searchlight's and Ijara's applicants can be compared to all mortgage and refinance loan applicants in the United States. Ijara is more similar to the aggregate data for all U.S. lenders than Searchlight, which has far more male applicants (table 4.3). Ijara's and Searchlight's applicants have slightly lower incomes (table 4.5). This may be an effect of their living in areas with higher median incomes, or it may be that, as anecdotally reported, truly wealthy Muslims prefer conventional (that is, non-Islamic) mortgages.

COMPARING THE CLIENT BASES OF THE TWO COMPANIES

Interesting differences emerge between the two companies when we look more closely at gender and income data by comparing the conditional odds of choosing one company over the other (tables 4.6 and 4.7). Those Muslims who applied for mortgages or refinancing loans jointly—that is, as husband and wife—were six times more likely to choose Ijara over Searchlight (odds ratio = 6.2). The results for income are less dramatic, but those Muslims with the highest incomes (120 percent or more of the median income in their MSA) were more than twice as likely to choose Ijara (odds ratio = 2.7). If we move from joint to single application for either sex, the odds of choosing Ijara over Searchlight decrease to 16 percent of what they had been for joint application status. If we move from the highest income level to the lowest (less than 50 percent of the median

TABLE 4.6   Conditional Odds of Choosing One Lender over the Other, by Gender, 2002 and 2003

	Female	Male	Joint
Ijara	0.28	0.28	1.76
Searchlight	3.52	3.46	0.57

Source: Author's compilation.

TABLE 4.7   Conditional Odds of Choosing One Lender over the Other, by Income, 2002 and 2003

	Less Than 50 Percent	50 to 79 Percent	80 to 99 Percent	100 to 119 Percent	120 Percent or More
Ijara	0.28	0.42	0.53	0.64	0.72
Searchlight	3.5	2.4	1.8	1.5	1.3

Source: Author's compilation.

income), the odds of choosing Ijara over Searchlight decrease to 37 percent of what they had been at the higher income level.

Loglinear analysis is a method of computing significance for contingency tables. It is more appropriate than methods like regression, analysis of variance, or factor analysis for the kind of data presented in HMDA reports because it permits tests of association and interaction for categorical data (data such as income *level* as opposed to actual numerical income). It also permits analysis of interactions between categorical variables—in this case, gender, income level, and company (on loglinear analysis of categorical data, see Agresti 1996).[7] A loglinear analysis attempts to eliminate variables and relationships between variables one by one so that ultimately a model with fewer variables or variable interactions than the actual contingency table can be created that most closely approximates the patterns of distribution of actual data.

Loglinear analysis of the frequency data for gender and income demonstrates that the relationships between gender and choice of company account for more of the distribution of the data than other factors, though income does account for some of it. All possible loglinear models were tested. When all of the available data were used, the homogenous association model best explained the distribution. In other words, all two-way effects between gender, income, and lender were necessary to account for the data (that is, a model based on the two-way effects gender × income, gender × lender, and income × lender is not significantly different from the saturated model that includes all possible one-way, two-way, and three-way effects). Since the homogenous model is not particularly parsimonious, loglinear analysis was conducted using only the cases where income was in the highest and lowest categories (120 percent or more and less than 50 percent). This had the same result: the homogenous association model best explained the distribution.

Using only those cases where income fell into the intermediate cate-

TABLE 4.8   Loglinear Analysis Conditional (Gender × Income)
             Independence Model: Goodness-of-Fit Tests

	Value	df	Significance
Likelihood ratio	7.075	8	.529
Pearson chi-square	7.243	8	.511

Source: Author's compilation.
Model: Poisson
Design: Constant + gender × lender + income × lender

gories can create more parsimonious models. Two models describe the data. With the lowest and highest income categories removed, a one-factor independence model with income held independent (income + gender × lender) is not significantly different from the saturated model (p = 0.066). This suggests that the two-way effect between gender and lender explains the distribution of the data. A stronger result is obtained with a conditional independence model that holds the effect between gender and income independent and uses gender × lender and income × lender to explain the distribution. This model is not significantly different from the saturated model (p = 0.511). This suggests that income is necessary to explain the distribution of the data in its relationship with lender, but not with its relationship with gender, combined with the two-way effect of gender and lender. Breaking down the model further, the combinations Ijara × 50–79%, Ijara × 80–99%, and Searchlight × 80–99% do not significantly contribute to the explanation of the distribution of the data. Male × Searchlight contributes most to the overall strength of the relationships in the data (Z = 16.73; see tables 4.8 and 4.9). This suggests that the real difference between the two applicant pools is the overrepresentation of single male applicants to Searchlight rather than the differences in income levels between applicants to the two companies.

Sieve and mosaic diagrams graphically represent the relationships between gender and income in the loglinear analysis (see Friendly 2000). Figure 4.1 is a mosaic diagram illustrating the relationship between gender and income for all mortgage and refinancing applicants in the United States in 2002 and 2003. The hatching indicates positive residuals, that is, more cases in a particular category than an equiprobable model would predict (and heavier hatching indicates higher positive residuals); dashed lines indicate negative residuals (fewer cases than expected). For example, the box in the lower left corner indicates that there is a higher-than-expected number of female applicants in the lowest income category. The

TABLE 4.9 Loglinear Analysis Conditional (Gender × Income) Independence Model: Parameter Estimates

Parameter	Estimate	Standard Error	Z	Significance	95 Percent Confidence Interval	
					Lower Bound	Upper Bound
Constant	3.696	.099	37.307	.000	3.502	3.891
[Gender = 0] × [lender = 1]	−1.866	.264	−7.078	.000	−2.382	−1.349
[Gender = 0] × [lender = 2]	−.856	.152	−5.650	.000	−1.154	−.559
[Gender = 1] × [lender = 1]	.501	.138	3.621	.000	.230	.773
[Gender = 1] × [lender = 2]	1.533	.091	16.793	.000	1.354	1.711
[Gender = 2] × [lender = 1]	.749	.134	5.581	.000	.486	1.012
[Gender = 2] × [lender = 2]	0a			—	—	—
[Income = 2] × [lender = 1]	.000	.113	.000	1.000	−.221	.221
[Income = 2] × [lender = 2]	.443	.082	5.400	.000	.282	.604
[Income = 3] × [lender = 1]	−.121	.116	−1.042	.297	−.348	.107
[Income = 3] × [lender = 2]	.064	.089	.713	.476	−.111	.238
[Income = 4] × [lender = 1]	0a			—	—	—
[Income = 4] × [lender = 2]	0a			—	—	—

Source: Author's compilation.
Model: Poisson
Design: Constant + gender × lender + income × lender
Notes: Lender 1 = Ijara; lender 2 = Searchlight; gender 0 = female; gender 1 = male; gender 2 = joint.
aSet to zero because it is redundant.

FIGURE 4.1   U.S. Mortgage Applicants by Gender and Income, 2002
and 2003

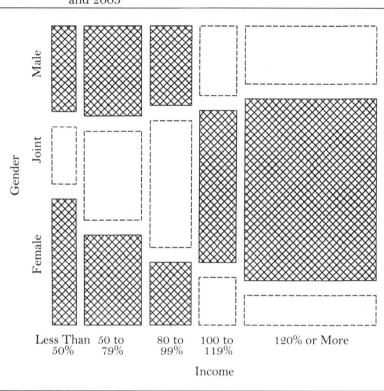

Source: Author's compilation.

box in the lower right corner indicates that there is a lower-than-expected number of female applicants in the highest income category. Figure 4.1 shows that there are high positive residuals for wealthier joint applicants and for poorer single applicants of either sex. This is not surprising: joint applicants with two incomes make more money than single applicants with one.

Figure 4.2 is a sieve diagram that shows comparisons between Ijara, Searchlight, and all U.S. lenders for income. Solid lines indicate positive residuals; dashed lines indicate negative residuals. For example, the box in the lower left corner indicates that there is a higher-than-expected number of applicants to Searchlight in the lowest income category; the box immediately above it indicates that there is a lower-than-expected number of applicants to Ijara in the lowest income category. Figure 4.2 shows Ijara's income profile to be more similar to that of all U.S. lenders,

FIGURE 4.2   Mortgage Applicants by Income, 2002 and 2003

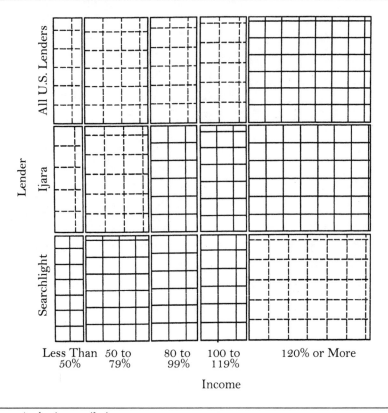

Source: Author's compilation.

with positive residuals in the highest income category. Searchlight has high positive residuals in all but the highest income category.

Finally, figure 4.3 is a mosaic diagram that illustrates the interactions between gender, income, and lender for Ijara and Searchlight. For example, the set of boxes in the lower right corner indicates that Ijara has fewer male applicants in the lowest income category than expected and that Searchlight has more male applicants in the lowest income category than expected. Figure 4.3 shows that Searchlight has positive residuals for male applicants from all income categories (though for the income category 100 to 119 percent of median income it is a low positive residual). Ijara has high positive residuals for joint applicants for all income categories. This is interesting because it suggests that joint couples of any income level choose Ijara over Searchlight and that income is less significant than gender category in accounting for the distribution of the data.

FIGURE 4.3   Lender, Gender, and Income, 2002 and 2003

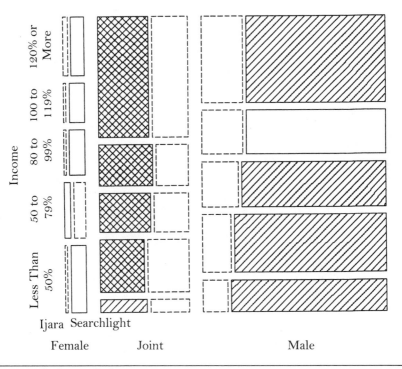

Source: Author's compilation.

A binomial logistic regression analysis paints a similar picture (table 4.10). If only gender is considered, the odds of choosing Searchlight over Ijara are 79.8 percent less if the application is joint. If gender and income are considered together, the poorer the applicant the greater the odds of choosing Searchlight (61 percent better for the lowest income category and 33 percent better for the second-lowest income category [see shaded rows on table 4.1]).

These analyses bear out the contrast between Searchlight's cohort of male applicants and Ijara's cohort of joint applicants, who may also be wealthier. There are a number of ways to explain the relationship between income and gender category. Married couples with two incomes are wealthier than single people with one. Yet many male Islamic mortgage applicants who apply singly are married. The wealthier couples may have more progressive views on marriage and finance, and they may take for granted that married couples jointly engage in financial activities like borrowing. Recalling from the loglinear analyses, however, that income

TABLE 4.10 Logistic Regression Analysis of Lender Choice

	B	Standard Error	Wald	df	Significance	Exp(B)	95.0 Percent Confidence Interval for Exp(B)	
							Lower	Upper
Step 1[a]								
Gender			273.542	2	.000			
Gender(1)	.102	.220	.214	1	.643	1.107	.719	1.705
Gender(2)	−1.599	.224	50.884	1	.000	.202	.130	.314
Constant	1.296	.210	38.254	1	.000	3.655		
Step 2[b]								
Gender			256.120	2	.000			
Gender(1)	.161	.222	.524	1	.469	1.174	.760	1.814
Gender(2)	−1.509	.227	44.074	1	.000	.221	.142	.345
IncCategory			10.633	4	.031			
IncCategory(1)	.476	.194	6.059	1	.014	1.610	1.102	2.353
IncCategory(2)	.290	.139	4.370	1	.037	1.336	1.018	1.754
IncCategory(3)	.097	.149	.429	1	.513	1.102	.823	1.476
IncCategory(4)	−.056	.146	.149	1	.700	.945	.710	1.259
Constant	1.120	.225	24.679	1	.000	3.063		

Source: Author's compilation.
[a] Variable(s) entered on step 1: gender.
[b] Variable(s) entered on step 2: IncCategory.
Gender (1) = Male

is not as necessary as gender to explain the distribution of the data, Ijara's poorer joint applicants may also have more progressive views on marriage and finance than Searchlight's poorer single applicants. Ijara thus may have a more progressive client base overall than Searchlight, regardless of income level.

This is one of the more provocative suggestions of the quantitative analysis presented in this chapter. Recall that Searchlight defines itself and its client base as more modern—even "postmodern"—and explicitly seeks clients who are not beholden to overly conservative or doctrinaire interpretations of Islamic law. Ijara, in contrast, advertises to "puritans." Yet Searchlight seems to attract more conservative applicants, and Ijara seems to attract more progressive applicants. At the same time, as discussed in the next chapter, some people I interviewed deemed Ijara's model to be *less* shari'a-compliant. Is this why more conservative Muslims choose Searchlight and more progressive Muslims choose Ijara? Does the client profile confirm the assessment of shari'a compliance? That is, is Ijara's more progressive applicant pool an indication that its product is in fact *less* shari'a-compliant, while Searchlight's more conservative applicant pool is proof that its product is *more* shari'a-compliant? Or could the potential applicant somehow be aware of the composition of Ijara's applicant pool in advance and thus decide that such applicants would naturally choose less compliant products? Confounding the matter further, consider the nature of the products each company offers and the manner in which they have crafted them. Ijara's lease-based product seems much more rigorously shari'a-compliant than Searchlight's profit-based one. How then does the assessment of whether a product is more or less shari'a-compliant figure into the strikingly different profiles of the applicants to these companies?

Perhaps we are asking the wrong questions of these mortgage alternatives and the data on their applicant pools. Perhaps progressive or conservative is not the best opposition to explain the differences among applicants and their approach to Islam's injunction against riba. And perhaps the implicit construction of shari'a as a kind of volumetric measure—one can have more or less of it—does not adequately capture the understandings and transformations of Islamic law occurring in the contemporary United States. The next chapters, which attempt to unpack this assertion, suggest an alternative way to view the differences between the two applicant pools, as well as the nature of shari'a compliance in American Islamic home financing.

CHAPTER FIVE

CHOOSING AN ISLAMIC MORTGAGE ALTERNATIVE

As the results reported in the previous chapter revealed, non-Muslim Americans' stereotypes of Muslims are not particularly helpful predictors of Muslim Americans' decisions and choices. This is true generally, of course. Nevertheless, I was puzzled by the quantitative data on the applicant pools for Islamic mortgages because they did not square with what I had learned from interviewing people involved in the business, including those charged with developing and marketing interest-free mortgage alternatives. If the "puritans" whom Ijara sought to serve were people whose everyday gender politics included patriarchal control over family resources—"traditional family values," in the current parlance in the United States—those puritans seemed to be choosing Searchlight instead.

Furthermore, as argued in chapter 3, there are some good reasons to consider Ijara's model more shari'a-compliant than Searchlight's: it is based on risk-sharing; it is firmly tied to rent, not an interest rate; and it has a clear exegetical warrant. If riba can be considered equivalent to medieval Christian usury, then, as a variation on the medieval vif-gage, it is non-usurious because the yield of the property for one co-owner, the client, can, if the client so chooses, be used to pay down the principal—although it does not have to be so used.

Furthermore, in interviews with southern California Muslims who either had applied for an Islamic mortgage or were considering it, I found that many, when asked to describe how an Islamic mortgage works—or how Islamic banking in general works—outlined something very close to Ijara's model. Lease-to-own contracts and/or mudaraba profit-and-loss-sharing contracts formed a sort of understood background to the whole discussion of Islamic banking. Diminishing musharaka co-owned enterprises or murabaha cost-plus markups were not contractual models that came easily to people, and they were never offered as an explanation or description of Islamic banking. I have found this to be the case in my broader research on Islamic banking, as have others, and it reflects the quasi-romantic attachment that people have for leasing and profit-and-loss sharing as the essential component of Islamic banking that demonstrates its commitment to fairness, justice, and equity despite the increasing ubiquity of other contractual forms (see El-Gamal 2000b; Maurer 2005; Saleh 1986). Ijara and mudaraba hold a special place in people's hearts; Saeed (1998) labels this attachment a trade-off between idealism and pragmatism.

As this chapter demonstrates, people have a fondness for ijara and mudaraba contracts—the latter of which has never been used for Islamic home financing in the United States—but are also strongly motivated by another set of concerns that have little to do with the Islamic part of Islamic banking. Those motivations help explain some people's preference for Searchlight's product. Ijara contracts feel processual, social, and collaborative, but people also strongly value anonymity, routine, and formality. In the interviews and participant-observation discussed in this chapter, anonymity and professionalism emerged as key selling points of Searchlight's Islamic mortgage products. And anonymity and professionalism were seen to go hand in hand. Although people value Islamic mortgages because they feel that such mortgages tie them to a community and an identity, they also equally value the asocial character of the bureaucracy and the formal and anonymous qualities of market exchange. Mortgages are like modern money itself then, in that they depersonalize transactions (Simmel 1907/1990) even as the transactions themselves are undertaken in the name of a deep social cum religious commitment to a community of believers.

Muslims seeking mortgages also insisted on seeing a product's seal of approval by prominent scholars. At the same time, they expected that seal of approval to come in a standardized form: they found a bureaucratic statement in legalese, with letterhead, signatures, and the like, more trustworthy than other means of communicating shari'a compliance. In a very important sense, then, people's understandings of "Islamic law" were shaped by their prior understandings of "law" itself. They understood law to be formal, rational, bureaucratic, and not based on personal ties. If an Islamic mortgage company could demonstrate that it operated in a formal, rational, bureaucratic, and impersonal manner, people understood it to be "lawful." Because it was an "Islamic" operation, they therefore understood it to be *Islamically* lawful.

This chapter quotes extensively from fifteen formal taped interviews and dozens of informal interviews and casual discussions with southern California Muslims and with professionals across the country involved in developing and marketing Islamic mortgage replacement products. At the start of this research, I relied more heavily on formal interviews. After a while, as usually happens, I found that I kept hearing the same things. Many people were quite frank, even on tape, but the tape recorder often intrudes, increases interviewer and interviewee self-consciousness, and stifles discussion. Formal interviews and informal conversations alike very often turned into "working discussions" in which together we tried to figure out precisely how a certain kind of contract might work in theory or in practice. In what follows, I attempt to convey the sense of those working discussions. Following the conventions of anthropology, I am interested here in the general discourse around Islamic banking and Islamic mortgage alternatives, not in treating each interviewee as a "subject" or "case" and then coding the data obtained in such a way as to permit me to conduct a statistical procedure like regression analysis. To understand the phenomenon of Islamic mortgages we need to listen in on the broad conversation that is taking place today in families, mosques, colleges, community organizations, and friendship networks. The ethnographic method is suited to providing a "thick description" (Geertz 1973) of that conversation; it also allows the researcher to return to those barely grasped moments during fieldwork that nag at him or her later on. Such moments provide the excess of data that is the hallmark of anthropological ethnography, as discussed in the introduction.

PRAGMATIC IDEALS

For Muslims seeking mortgage alternatives, the ideal often *is* the pragmatic. Even Searchlight clients described their mortgage alternative as a rent-to-own contract. Here is how one Searchlight customer explained it:

> It's kind of like a rent-to-own-type thing. . . . They co-own with us, as if it were owning it with somebody, like another human being or

something. Where we kind of own part of the house with them and it's like a rent-to-own, we kind of pay them, like, you know, rent to own it basically. That's just how it seemed like and made sense to me.

Her husband added: "With, like, profit-sharing as well . . . so pay rent plus, like, profit." Profit sharing is the key element of mudaraba, a profit-and-loss-sharing contract in Islamic banking that many professionals and clients alike assume to be the foundation of the entire field. But mudaraba is not one of the contractual forms taken by Islamic mortgages in the United States.

Another interviewee who had researched both companies but decided against refinancing with either one explained the whole field of Islamic banking this way:

All right. So the idea of just borrowing money and paying back more just for the sake of having a premium on the loan is haram [forbidden], riba-wise. But if you do it in terms of, like, an invest[ment], like a possible risk where you win or lose and the person loaning the money will either make a profit with you as the borrower or lose money with you if you [lose] money, and then for him it's an invest[ment] either way—he can go up or down—so in that sense it's halal.

He then explained how he thought Ijara's model works: "They're getting more money, kind of like the bank gets more money by interest, but it's legitimized by saying that this is the rent, fair market rent of the house that you're paying them, and [so] it's not just money for money."

Almost everyone, in fact, not only understood the ijara component of Ijara's mortgage alternative but also understood leasing and profit-and-loss sharing to be the centerpiece of what makes Islamic banking "Islamic" and what makes it superior to conventional interest-based finance:

Islamically, it's cool to loan somebody money as an investment and say, you know, we're both gonna buy this house together, and if it makes money, then we both make money, and if it loses money, then we both lose money, because that's fair, 'cause there's a risk involved for both people, as opposed to being like a loan shark where, you know, I'm gonna give you a hundred dollars and you have to pay me a hundred and ten, [and] I don't care if, you know, your business goes under or whatever happens, you know, you have to pay me this much money, and that's the way it is.

At the same time, however, many interviewees believed that Ijara's model was *identical* to Searchlight's. Of the latter this interviewee said, "You rent the house from them while you pay part of the equity and part of the rent in each payment." Indeed, there was some confusion over Searchlight's so-called profit payment. Some considered it an administrative fee, others described it as a fee for a service, and still others thought of it as identical to the rent payment. Many either considered it a combination of these or could not decide over the course of the interview what exactly the profit payment was or how it was determined.

WHAT'S THE DIFFERENCE?

People debated the difference between Ijara and Searchlight as well as the difference between Islamic financing and conventional financing. Many did not see any differences at all. Most were familiar with the Qaradawi fatwa that ruled that interest-based mortgages are permissible in cases of necessity, even if they could not recall the shaykh's name. One interviewee explained:

> Shaykh Yusuf al-Qaradawi had given a fatwa that it's okay to buy a house with interest if it's the house to house your family and put a roof over their head, because that takes precedence over whether or not you're dealing with interest because you have to provide for your family home and make sure that they're taken care of.

People understood at least one restriction, however, on the use of an interest-based loan for a home purchase:

> [This] doesn't mean that you can go and buy houses and rent them out and make money off them with interest, because that's not a fard [obligation], like, that's not a necessity to take care of your family.

> So long as it's for your home [and] it's not like you're going to buy things with interest so that you can go rent it out and make a bunch of money or for investment issues or for anything else.

For many, reference to the Qaradawi fatwa reinforced their belief that one should turn to "well-respected scholars," as one put it, to settle questions of shari'a. Such scholars, by issuing rulings, can make things like interest payments "Islamically okay":

> There's a lot of scholars that have made it Islamically okay to buy a house on interest, because they say the fard of putting a home, a roof, over your family's home is more important than worrying about the shari'a issues of whether or not you should pay interest.

That some respected scholars have declared interest-based mortgages permissible for the purpose of providing a home for one's family has convinced some Muslims that it is not incumbent on them to adhere to the prohibition of interest at all. Some expressed frustration with what they saw as a lack of consensus among scholars about "this riba stuff." Some teased their friends or family members who, they believed, worried excessively about the status of riba, about whether interest is riba, and about whether, for example, credit cards and student loans are permissible. Still others argued that, since there are opportunities for people with "good credit" to avoid interest, they should take advantage of non-riba-based financing when it is available to them but not worry about it so much when it is not.

> Q: Say, when you actually take out a loan, like a school loan or something ... like, which company would you go with, or would you even go with, like, Islamic corporations for home mortgages?
>
> A: Honestly, if I had to deal with a loan for a house or car or something ... I would rather avoid all that mess and go buy like a Ford at zero percent interest, 'cause you could just avoid it altogether instead of trying to decide whether or not this is halal or haram.

Some felt that it is better to avoid issues of shari'a whenever possible, especially if doing so might save money in the long run:

> The bottom line is, as an individual you don't want to be spending a ton more money to do something halal when there's an option of zero percent interest where you would save yourself a ton of money and not have to worry about this whole Islamic law issue to begin with.

The analogy to zero-percent-interest automobile financing breaks down for home financing, since zero-percent-interest conventional mortgages do not exist. But for some people skepticism about Islamic banking, together with the Qaradawi fatwa and the belief that conventional mortgages are cheaper, led them to reject Islamic mortgages altogether.

Skepticism about Islamic banking took the form of questions about the precise nature of profit-and-loss sharing. Many people wondered whether and how the Islamic mortgage company would take a loss if the rental value of the property decreased. People thought that if the company took a loss, then it would be "really shari'a," or "really halal." "If it's a two-way street"—that is, if both parties to the contract could lose money—"then it would be *really* halal."

> A: But I'm saying, that's the difference between halal . . . if it's a two-way street, because if they could lose on the deal . . .
>
> B: Yeah, exactly.
>
> A: . . . along with you, then it's okay, but if they don't lose, then I think the whole thing is just . . .
>
> B: A front.
>
> A: . . . biased.

Those who were more inclined to accept the legitimacy and necessity of Islamic banking, saw a difference between Islamic and conventional mortgages, and sought the former over the latter tended not to view the various mortgage replacement products available as different from one another. Almost everyone had heard of Ijara or Searchlight. Many knew both and knew of some of the others available as well. Those who had heard of both thought that their products were essentially the same and that they were ijara-based lease-to-own contracts. "I looked into both Searchlight and Ijara," one interviewee stated, "and I found that the policies of both companies are very similar." "They're just two different companies doing the same thing." In sum, people thought that the products offered by each were identical.

THE SHARI'A SCHOLAR SEAL OF APPROVAL

So why choose one mortgage replacement product over the other? People cited two factors, and these two factors usually worked in Searchlight's favor: perceived cost and perceived level of shari'a compliance. Most people thought Ijara's mortgage alternative would end up costing them more than Searchlight's. "There really is no difference" between the two, one person said. "It's just that one is a little cheaper than the other." Speaking of Ijara, another person said, "I think the way it turned out was that our mortgage was, like, going to pretty much, like, double if we were going to go with them."

The issue of shari'a compliance came up quite a bit in discussions about the difference between the two companies. Those who had an opinion tended to think that Searchlight was more shari'a-compliant than Ijara. Their reasons were at first confusing to me, because many of the same people who expressed doubts about Ijara also stated that its product was identical to Searchlight's. Of course, there are differences between the products. But it was not an assessment of the products themselves that led people to see Searchlight as more compliant. It was their assessment of the scholars and shaykhs who were believed to have endorsed each company, and an elision between the idea of endorsement and the idea of a universality or global reach that was afforded to Searchlight but not to Ijara.

"We wanted to make sure we did something Muslim," one woman stated. "Ijara hasn't been approved by a lot of shaykhs." People cited Shaykh M. Taqi Usmani of Pakistan and the American shaykh Yusuf Talal de Lorenzo. "Well, I mean, I don't know if they particularly *didn't* endorse Ijara, but they didn't . . . it wasn't a public endorsement. But with Searchlight, like, all these scholars publicly endorsed it."

Searchlight's website and application packet contain copies of the fatwas issued by its shari'a supervisory board, with the signatures of famous and well-respected shari'a scholars and shaykhs prominently displayed. One couple explained:

> A: Actually, even in our loan application—
>
> B: —there was like a written, ummm . . .
>
> A: . . . yeah, there's like a page just with their endorsement—
>
> B: —just saying it's part of the application.
>
> A: Yeah, it's proof to the consumers that this is legit as far as we're concerned.

People were impressed with the caliber of the scholars who endorsed Searchlight's product. "He's like a world-renowned faqih [jurist] and stuff, and he's, like, really hard-line . . . when it comes to things like riba."

People also relied on their friends for advice, especially friends who were "against riba." Friends advised them to look for products with "a lot of backing." Indeed, the word *backing* or other terms expressing an anterior warrant came up a lot in my informal conversations with Muslims in southern California. People made comments about Searchlight such as, "It's got good people behind it," or, "It's really got a lot of backing." That anterior warrant translated into global reach. Despite Ijara's broader national reach (see table 4.1), almost everyone I talked to identified Ijara as a "California" company and Searchlight as "national" or as "everywhere." People had had broad exposure to Searchlight's marketing materials, and some had met representatives of the company at conferences. "They're everywhere!" said one interviewee. "Searchlight is at every single conference, at every single event." Of Ijara, people said, "You don't really see them anywhere." Searchlight, by contrast, has "crossed the nation."

People also felt that Searchlight was "more professional" or "more organized." People cited with approval the formality and professionalism of the paperwork they were required to fill out. "They even did credit checks!" "They looked at all our W2s." People were *pleased* that Searchlight did not "trust" them as potential clients but required all the information a traditional lender would demand. In contrast to mortgage scholar Ann Burkhart's (1999) lament that the nationalization and standardization of the mortgage business has led to ever-decreasing social connections—and therefore social obligations—between lenders and the communities in which they operate, those I spoke with had exactly the opposite assessment of the quasi-anonymous quality of their relationship with Searchlight. They appreciated being catered to as Muslims. But they also appreciated being treated "like, as a real *client,* or something" as one put it to me. Muslim companies, it was thought, were too lackadaisical or overly trusting of other Muslims. Not Searchlight. "It wasn't like traditional . . . Muslim companies, 'Oh, it's okay, just let it go, whatever.'" Professionalism here meant anonymity achieved through bureaucratic rationality. People preferred the formality of bureaucratic and market mechanisms that made them anonymous—and indeed, that gave them no advantages even for being Muslim. If being Muslim meant getting a break from a Muslim company, such potential clients rejected the enterprise as suspect.

Ijara has essentially the same paperwork as Searchlight. In fact, with Freddie Mac involvement in the Islamic mortgage business, almost all Islamic home financing companies now use standard Freddie Mac mortgage application forms. Every company does credit checks, and all require W2s and other proofs of income and continued employment. And of course, considering the quantitative data presented in the previous chapter, Searchlight has not in fact crossed the nation. Ijara has. Its distribution of clients, while not as deep in any particular area, is much wider than Searchlight's.

The decision to choose either Ijara or Searchlight seems to have little to do with the actual product. People think that the products are the same—that they are both ijara contracts. The choice also has little to do with the interpretation of the product. People think ijara contracts are *"really* shari'a."* People mistakenly believe that Searchlight has a *"really* shari'a" ijara-based product. But what makes many choose Searchlight over Ijara is neither its product nor its shari'a status, but the *public* backing of prominent scholars. This may explain the gender differences between applicants to each company. Those who choose Searchlight are not necessarily more "conservative" but may hold a particular understanding of Islamic law. Islamic law, for them, must look like "law" in the abstract sense. In chapter 8, I argue that this interpretation of Islamic law as requiring the public and formally bureaucratic backing of prominent scholars may represent a transformation of shari'a in the United States, where charisma is less important than bureaucratic rationality.

Achieving the backing of prominent scholars and thereby having the weight of an anterior warrant issued by such figures creates the illusion that Searchlight has a national presence. Scholars of global significance have endorsed the product, so the product must have a wider reach than Ijara's. "Wider reach" translates into "more shari'a-compliant," since shari'a is supposed to be universally applicable. The illusion of national coverage also means formal anonymity—the anonymity of the nation-form itself, the anonymous horizontal solidarity of the "imagined community" that Benedict Anderson (1983) characterized as having been forged through public print media like newspapers. Here the public print media are bureaucratically rendered in the form of publicly available fatwas and standardized Freddie Mac application forms. Anonymity also translates into professionalism. Muslims debating mortgages are creating a world that brings into alignment standardized print media, public endorsements of prominent figures, and universal reach. It is something that resembles Islam itself: a standard, unalterable, and untranslatable written text, chains of exegetical authority via hadith, and the universality of Islam expressed in the global horizontal solidarity of the umma, the global community of believers.

But it is paradoxically indeterminate as well. Shari'a contains apparent anomalies like the Qaradawi fatwa, which leaves open the permissibility of interest-based mortgages. This open-endedness resembles nothing so much as Ijara's mortgage product, the rent payments of which are continually revisable in accordance with the property's living and ever-changing yield. Muslims for whom shari'a is about human attempts to approach God through such continual revision may thus find Ijara's product more compliant—or at least more reflective of the workings of what they see as the divinely inspired universe whose imperfections were scripted in advance.

In an important study of authority and change in Islamic law, Wael Hallaq (2001, 238) argues that the narrowing of juristic possibilities that occurred in the ninth and tenth centuries A.D. (or third and fourth centuries A.H.) constituted a transition from the age of ijtihad to the age of taqlid, or imitation. But, he demonstrated, taqlid is not simply the "unquestioning acceptance of earlier positions" but is itself "a juristic activity of the first order" that "involve[s] highly complex modes of legal reasoning and rhetorical discourse." Instead of becoming a deadening process of legal copying, taqlid is more an effect of the invention of new modes of authority, which in the ninth and tenth centuries A.D. congealed in the institutionalization of schools of jurisprudence. Hallaq shows that even as this institutionalization reduced juristic plurality and "increased determinacy and predictability," it also, paradoxically, was a tool of legal change and transformation: "In the very act of declaring certain opinions as authoritative, legal change" took place (239). Within the limits of the schools of fiqh, the jurist "constantly adduced new arguments from old materials" (241).

As in the ninth century, so today there is a dialectical interaction between ijtihad and taqlid. That dialectic is being worked out in people's everyday debates over shari'a as well as in corporate duels over the status of financial contracts and shari'a scholars' supervision of Islamic mortgages and other financial products. Shari'a's finality and its determinacy are undergirded by its flexibility and pluralism. As the foregoing chapters have demonstrated, however, Searchlight and Ijara cannot neatly be placed in either the "determinacy" or "flexibility" box. I return to this subject in chapter 8.

CHAPTER SIX

THE SECURITIZATION OF ISLAMIC MORTGAGES

On March 8, 2004, at a conference at the Crowne Plaza Hotel in Dubai, the Guidance Financial Group launched the first American Islamic mortgage-backed security product. The Guidance Fixed Income Fund is a mutual fund that holds securities backed by Guidance's real estate financing assets. Freddie Mac issues the securities. As a press release reported:

> A first rate issuer, a superior credit rating, and deep liquidity characterize the new securities held by Guidance. Most important, these securities introduce to the Islamic capital markets both investment instruments that currently trade in the U.S. mortgage-backed securities market and the benefits of those instruments.
>
> "Freddie Mac mortgage-backed securities not only provide an efficient way to enhance returns with limited volatility, they also benefit from a favorable treatment in terms of capital adequacy requirements," said Dr. Hasnita Hashim, a Managing Director of the Guidance Financial Group. . . . "We hope that introducing such assets would contribute to the efficiency of the Islamic banking sector." (AME Info.com 2004)

The press release also reported that Guidance had originated mortgages worth over $200 million and that, in partnership with Freddie Mac, it had developed a "soundly designed distribution process."

This chapter reflects on the introduction of Islamic mortgage-backed securities (MBS). The creation of shari'a-compliant security instruments is an effort to tap into the capital of global Muslim investors who either have stayed out of securities markets because of injunctions against interest or, much more frequently, have invested in conventional securities but would choose an Islamic "brand" if one were available. The creation of Islamic mortgage-backed securities opens up new sources of capital for the Islamic mortgage market. It also leads to new questions, such as whether Freddie Mac involvement in the endeavor taints the purity of the products—since Freddie Mac is an American government-sponsored enterprise—or whether it is even permissible to create securities in mortgages in the first place. Importantly, however, securitization has meant increasing standardization and a new kind of global reach. This, in turn, has important implications for people's everyday understandings of the market in which they are participating when they take out an Islamic mortgage, as well as for scholarly conceptions of the market itself as a social process.

Recall from chapter 1 that the purpose of Freddie Mac and other government-sponsored enterprises involved in home financing in the United States is to generate liquidity for real estate lending. They do so by bundling individual mortgages together into large pools and selling shares in the pools. Investors seeking a return on their money can invest in MBS, while potential home buyers benefit from a continual flow of capital into the real estate financing market. The U.S. Securities and Exchange Commission (SEC) provides a helpful explanation:

> Mortgage-backed securities (MBSs) are debt obligations that represent claims to the cash flows from pools of mortgage loans, most commonly on residential property. Mortgage loans are purchased from banks, mortgage companies, and other originators and then assembled into pools by a governmental, quasi-governmental, or private entity. The entity then issues securities that represent claims on the principal and interest payments made by borrowers on the loans in the pool, a process known as securitization.
>
> Most MBSs are issued by the Government National Mortgage Association (Ginnie Mae), a U.S. government agency, or the Federal National Mortgage Association (Fannie Mae) and the Federal Home Loan Mortgage Corporation (Freddie Mac), U.S. government-sponsored enterprises. Ginnie Mae, backed by the full faith and credit of the U.S. government, guarantees that investors will receive timely

payments. Fannie Mae and Freddie Mac also provide certain guarantees and, while not backed by the full faith and credit of the U.S. government, have special authority to borrow from the U.S. Treasury. Some private institutions, such as brokerage firms, banks, and homebuilders, also securitize mortgages, known as "private-label" mortgage securities.[1]

There have been a handful of Islamic security issuances globally. Guidance's is significant because it represents the first Islamic security backed by U.S. real estate paper. Malaysia, Qatar, and the Islamic Development Bank (IDB) have each issued Islamic securities under a contractual structure called a sukuk, a very recent innovation in Islamic banking that does not predate the 2000s. The term in Arabic is simply the plural form of the word for a deed or legal document (sakk), much like an MBS is, in a sense, a concatenation of a plurality of mortgage documents. Malaysia offered the first sukuk in 2002 backed by ijara contracts; Qatar followed in 2003. The IDB sukuk included ijara contracts as well as interests in murabaha (cost-plus) and istisna (construction or manufacturing) contracts (see Cole and Al-Sheikh 2004).

Creating security interests in such contracts involves understanding them as both partible and negotiable. That is, one must conceptualize the contracts as divisible into separate units that can be disaggregated and reaggregated into new units, and one must conceptualize the contracts as able to be signed over (negotiated) to other people or entities (see Maurer 1999). They must be fungible, transactable, and not forever tied to the tangible asset around which they were created in the first place or to the two parties to the original contract built around that tangible asset. Leasing contracts have generally been understood to be negotiable because they constitute interests in an underlying tangible asset. Furthermore, those interests are not based on a delay in time but are calculated on the spot, as it were. The rent is calculated by marking to market in real time (in theory, if not in practice). Murabaha and istisna contracts, which represent interests in a "stream of payments" rather than an underlying asset, have not been understood to be negotiable (Cole and al-Sheikh 2004, 2). Both are forms of markup or cost-plus payments made in return for the delayed completion of the contract. Because the markup resembles a payment for the use of money for a period of time, murabaha and istisna seem much closer to interest-bearing loans. The difference is that the markup is preset at the beginning of the contract and does not (in theory) change.

Shari'a scholars have tended to view any contract that departs too far from the tangible asset originally animating it as potentially subject to an illegitimate increase in value, or riba, because the increase comes about through a deferment or delay in the complete execution of the contract. Consider a conventional mortgage. The contract is complete when the mortgage is paid off and (in the Littletonian sense, from chapter 1) the gage, or pledge, "dies." For Islamic finance, any activity involving the contract between the time of its inception and the time of its completion that creates an increase in value is suspect because that increase comes about through the deferment in time of the contract's completion.[2] For ijara leases, the income generated for the lender does not come about because of the deferment of the contract's completion, but because of the rents from the "living" property in real time, as in a medieval vif-gage, except that those profits are not used to pay down the loan principal (unless, as previously discussed, the borrower chooses to use the portion of the rent he or she pays to himself or herself to pay down the principal).

To accommodate the inclusion of murabaha and istisna contracts in the IDB's sukuk, the shari'a scholars who authorized the product insisted that ijara contracts make up at least 25 percent of the portfolio (Cole and Al-Sheikh 2004, 2; see also AME Info.com 2004). When the sukuk was first issued, ijara contracts constituted 66 percent of its assets (Cole and Al-Sheikh 2004, 2). Thus, as we have seen in previous chapters, ijara contracts continue to pull on the imagination of Islamic finance. Here that pull is turned into a mathematical calculus.

If the presence of ijara contracts in sukuks assuages the "idealism" side in the idealism versus pragmatism debate in Islamic banking discussed by Saeed (1998), other aspects of the creation of secondary markets in Islamic financial contracts, like Guidance's mortgage replacement products, make some people nervous. For one thing, some of the early experiments in securitization took place in offshore financial service centers and in Switzerland. Faisal Finance Switzerland (FFS) securitized its real estate and equipment leases in the 1990s. In a white paper posted on Guidance's website, a former associate of FFS recommends that "Islamic international investors investing in the USA . . . set up . . . in a tax-free jurisdiction like the Channel Islands or in a country with a tax-treaty with the USA like Ireland or Luxembourg" (Abdi Dualeh 1998, 4).

Second, some of the professionals to whom I talked in the course of this research, as well as many more who are involved in the online and face-to-face debates in the worlds of Islamic banking and finance, express skepticism about securitization. First, they see it as coming very close to the line in terms of shari'a compliance because it is a further abstraction from the tangible assets on which contracts like ijara or diminishing musharaka are supposed to be based. Securitization represents another level of abstraction and a greater degree of distance from real property. Muslims should deal not in imaginary paper or intangible assets, but "in real things," one Islamic banker told me. Interest in such intangibles, he held, is in itself a form of interest. For some, the Islamic banking community's turn toward capital markets represents a turn away from the needs of Muslims: pragmatism—and greedy pragmatism to boot—is prevailing over idealism. "It becomes just another business investment," lamented an elderly convert long interested in the utopian promise of Islamic banking.

Third, as one professional put it, the activity around securitizing Islamic assets is "not a grassroots movement." People see it as having the potential to make a lot of money and to earn good returns on the investments of the already wealthy, but they do not see it as directly benefiting "everyday Muslims" who wish simply to provide for their families. "They are doing this hoping that they can get the paper [the mortgage paper, the sakk] and then securitize it and then sell it to an Islamic bank in the Gulf and make a spread on it," as one professional put it. "It's an economic interest," he suggested, and a marketing gimmick to attract new investment capital. Skepticism about securitization interacts with skepticism about a common figure in these debates: the "Gulf States," "the wealthy Arabs in the Gulf," or "money men offshore."

Fourth, some American Muslims are skeptical about securitization for another reason. Even though Islamic MBS cannot be bought in this country, those who knew about Freddie Mac involvement often suspected that the U.S. government is meddling in the financial affairs of American Muslims or that American Islamic finance companies are too closely tied with the government. As one professional related, after Freddie Mac became involved in the Islamic mortgage business, "some people said, 'Hey, why is the United States government helping you?'" There is wide discussion among people interested in Islamic banking of the issue of "mixing" funds from one source with funds from another that might not be operating in a manner consistent with shari'a or the interests of Muslims generally. Here, Freddie Mac money is seen as "American government money," or "Uncle Sam's money"—the same money that has been funding wars in the Middle East and supporting both the state of Israel and Middle Eastern kings and dictators. Knowledge of Freddie Mac involvement, coupled with skepticism about the intentions of the U.S. government vis-à-vis its relations with both the Muslim world and its own Muslim citizens, has led some to stay out of the Islamic mortgage market altogether.

Several Islamic finance companies post information about Freddie Mac involvement on their websites or in their marketing material to address these concerns. Guidance, for example, responds in this way to one "Common Question" about its declining balance co-ownership program: "Does Guidance utilize external funding for the Program?"

> The Declining Balance Co-ownership Program has been designed to comply with Shari'a principles from A to Z—from the point when a customer enters a home financing transaction to the point where the ultimate financing for that transaction is provided. Guidance obtains external funding for the Program through an agreement with Freddie Mac, a corporation chartered by Congress to support the home financing market. In this agreement, Freddie Mac makes investments to take a co-ownership stake in properties financed under the Program. At a second stage, Freddie Mac creates Shari'a-compliant securities invested in the co-ownership assets. These securities will be offered by Guidance to Islamic banks and other Islamic capital market participants around the world. These securities constitute a significant innovation that contributes to the development of the international Islamic financial market. (Guidance Financial 2004, 5)

The co-ownership element of Guidance's product is replicated at every level of scale, from the relationship with the potential client to Guidance's relationship with Freddie Mac, to Freddie Mac's relationship with the Islamic capital market.

Thus, one response to the skepticism is that securitization *does* benefit "everyday Muslims" by injecting capital and stability into the Islamic mortgage market. As a representative from Freddie Mac argued in an interview, "It all goes to the core of what Freddie Mac was set up to do—to bring some efficiencies to the broader market and to allow all Americans to take advantage of an efficient and effective mortgage market sector." Speaking of Islamic mortgage-backed securities, he noted that they serve two needs simultaneously: the needs of those who want a shari'a-compliant way to purchase a home and the needs of those who want securities that are "100 percent" made up of Islamically acceptable assets. Other professionals echoed the great importance of Freddie Mac involvement in providing home financing alternatives for American Muslims. For Freddie Mac, investing in Islamic mortgages is a "drop in the bucket," one shari'a scholar told me, but "what has been done up until [Freddie Mac involvement] is minuscule." Furthermore, Freddie Mac fosters the growth of "national organizations" that "will actually be competitive" with conventional mortgage brokers. Where once an applicant might have had to wait six or eight months to get an Islamic mortgage, now "it'll be a matter of a couple of days." Previously, Islamic finance companies had to rely on local or regional investors to support their enterprises. Those investors were often former business partners, members of extensive family and friendship networks, or the occasional conference-goer who heard a presentation on the company and decided to put some money into it. Freddie Mac involvement and now Islamic MBS will, it is hoped, permit an unprecedented scalability of Islamic mortgage alternatives.

In addition, promoters of Islamic securities argue that by providing a shari'a-compliant MBS to Middle Eastern investors, they help to promote transparency and good governance in that part of the world. "The Middle East and the Muslim world are unfortunately still terribly shot through with corruption," a shari'a scholar told me, yet by providing opportunities for truly Islamically permissible investments, American Islamic finance companies are promoting not only piety and the ethical precepts of Islam but also the capitalist virtues of accountability, transparency, and efficiency, which another professional characterized as "the values we all hold most dear."

Marketing and selling American Islamic MBS in the Middle East may have other virtues as well. Getting the "wealthy Gulf guys" to invest in American Muslims gives them a stake in the United States and a commitment to its economic success. The regions are thus tied closer together, not through oil, war, or political conflict but through a simple act of domesticity—buying a house to call home. And it does so through U.S. government–sponsored enterprises like Freddie Mac, which is viewed by most involved as fair, reputable, safe, and neutral.

At the end of the last chapter, I suggested that standardization had paradoxical effects. It permits the kind of anonymity that conjures universality, global reach, and solidarity through the imagined community of horizontal ties of equal citizenship. It also underwrites particularity and perpetual revisability: if we have a standard form for something, we can play around within the spaces on the form or at the margins (see Riles 1998). That play may lead us to want to revise the form itself. In the case of Islamic MBS, the standardization brought about by the participation of U.S. government–sponsored enterprises like Freddie Mac has enabled another kind of global reach—one that stretches to the Gulf states and redirects capital toward U.S. real estate financing that may have sat idle or been invested elsewhere. This new global reach conjures the universality of the market as well as the infinitely divisible market niches that constitute it and reauthorize it for those who may once have sought to stand outside it, almost like the infinite partibility and universal negotiability of mortgage paper itself.

CHAPTER SEVEN

HOME FINANCING AND THE TRANSFORMATION OF AMERICAN ISLAMIC LAW

Dale Eickelman and Jon Anderson (1999, 12) report that emerging Muslim leaders are "presenting Islamic doctrine and discourse in accessible, vernacular terms" by using "styles of reasoning and forms of argument that draw on wider and less exclusive or erudite bodies of knowledge" (see also Leonard 2003, 20). Karen Leonard (2003) and Khaled Abou El Fadl (1998) note that, in the field of fiqh, the tendency in the United States has been for self-declared experts to make proclamations based on very weak attachments to particular schools or methods of Islamic jurisprudential reasoning. The gate of ijtihad, or individual interpretation of the sources of Islamic law, seems wide open in the United States—or at least open to self-styled experts or emerging and increasingly professionalized leaders. Where does the field of Islamic home mortgage alternatives fit in this picture, and what is its impact on the development of Islamic law in the United States?

As noted in chapters 4 and 5, Muslim Americans are far from unanimous on the question of Islamic mortgages. For some, the prohibition of interest is a trivial concern; the necessity of providing a home for one's family trumps whatever trepidation they may have toward interest. For others, the possibility of rendering a transaction interest-free (through creative household budgeting that sets income from other assets against interest payments, for example) makes the question moot.[1] Those who are seeking interest-free alternatives to conventional mortgages are themselves far from uniform on which company's product is better or more shari'a-compliant, and as shown in chapter 4, there are some striking differences between the applicant pools of two popular companies. These differences may have to do with differences in interpretation of Islamic precepts and may reflect broader debates in Islamic jurisprudence over the interplay of doctrine, juristic rulings, imitation, and individual interpretation, as discussed at the end of chapter 5.

In a posting of December 26, 2004, to the IBFNet Internet listserv, one of the predominant discussion forums for Islamic banking and finance globally, Dr. Muhammad Anas Zarka of the International Investor Company in Kuwait argued that the plurality of shari'a, while sometimes confusing, is nonetheless necessary and beneficial to the growth of Islamic finance:

> All Shari'a Boards I know of, including ours at The International Investor Co., Kuwait, and the International Fiqh Academy of OIC [Organization of the Islamic Conference], Jeddah, do not restrict their fatwas in financial transactions to the rulings of any particular school of fiqh. They have the capacity and authority to choose a prior fiqh ruling from one school or the other, or exercise fresh ijtihad (original juristic ruling) not bound by the prior fiqh rulings of any school. This gives rise to Multiplicity and Variance. . . . Believe it or not, top Muslim jurists old and new have maintained Multiplicity to be a singular advantage. Islamic fiqh is a pluralist not a monolithic body of knowledge.

At the same time, Dr. Zarka continued, such multiplicity can be a barrier to Islamic finance's global reach because it can confuse consumers and hinder standardization:

> To many practitioners of Islamic finance and to the public at large Multiplicity is frankly a potential source of confusion. More seriously, it is a hurdle to establishing common standards for the industry. . . . The need for common standards in [the] Islamic finance industry is undeniable, no matter how much we value multiplicity and pluralism in fatwas. Common standards are essential to promote honest competition and permit comparability of financial performance of different institutions. Can we achieve this without trying the impossible unification of fatwas? I think we can.

Dr. Zarka's proposal involves asking independent shari'a supervisory boards of Islamic finance companies to submit annual reports to the Accounting and Auditing Organization for Islamic Financial Institutions (AAOIFI) detailing any fatwas they have issued and the manner in which they were arrived at. This would preserve multiplicity but also ensure oversight.

In the United States, as noted in chapter 2, there has been a convergence of expertise in Islamic mortgage financing and shari'a supervision and scholarship. Prominent American and international shari'a scholars sit on the supervisory boards of several Islamic mortgage companies. As already noted, some see in this the potential for a conflict of interest. Many clients, on the other hand, not only accept but embrace the involvement of prominent shari'a scholars in Islamic mortgage companies. For them, standardized forms, Freddie Mac participation, national reach, and a new imagined public sphere go hand in hand with the interpretive underwriting of important shaykhs. As shown in chapter 5, prior "backing" by shari'a scholars gives an Islamic mortgage product added legitimacy and exegetical heft. This is the case even if the product seems to be less compliant than other mortgage alternatives. The creation by some shari'a supervisory boards of a standard form in which to record the fatwas themselves formalizes the fatwa both literally and figuratively. (Often included in mortgage application packets, the form is printed on letterhead, has signatures at the bottom, and looks and feels like a "legal" document.) People place their trust and their faith in these forms.

One way to interpret this formalization of rulings by prominent shari'a experts (whether or not one considers them "self-appointed," as critics charge) is in terms of Max Weber's (1968) famous discussion of the routinization of charismatic authority. Weber argued that there had been a shift in religious and political legitimacy—from tradition to charisma to formal legality—that reflected the increasing rationalization of modern society. Charismatic authority relies on "devotion to the exceptional sanctity, heroism or exemplary character of an individual person, and of the normative patterns or order revealed or ordained by him" (Weber 1968, 215). When the charismatic leader dies, charisma can be routinized and depersonalized through hereditary succession, the emergence of virtuosity or skill among the new leaders who pick up the charismatic mantle, or the institutionalization of charisma through the creation of offices or posts held by those who would claim authority in the name of the charismatic leader. Institutionalized office charisma can feed into rational-legal modes of legitimacy and a gradual secularization of the sources of authority. We could easily craft a history of Islamic jurisprudence that begins with the Prophet's revelations, continues through the virtuosity or hereditary charisma of the companions of the Prophet, and leads to the emergence of schools of jurisprudence based on hadith, or stories from the life of the Prophet related by his companions and passed down through chains of scholars. Contemporary shari'a scholars are the most recent links in those chains of authority. Shari'a supervisory boards and the standardized forms for fatwas that are submitted for review to an international agency like the AAOIFI represent the institutionalization of charisma through bureaucratic offices and a blending of charismatic and rational-legal forms of authority. Islamic finance has thus spurred the institutionalization of charismatic authority; American Islamic home mortgages raise this institutionalization to another level by fostering the implementation of universally applicable modes of interpretation and universally extendible, standardized forms and procedures. More locally, Islamic banking companies that rely on the charisma of a handful of founders lose market share to those that rely on increasingly institutionalized shari'a supervisory boards that attach themselves to these universally extendible forms all the way up a new chain of bureaucratic authority to the AAOIFI.

As noted in the introduction, to some critics like Timur Kuran (2004), Islamic banking is part of a neorevivalist ideological project that has contributed to anti-Western and antimodern sentiment in the Muslim world. They see it as based on literalist interpretations of classic texts and founded in faulty economics. Kuran echoes Fazlur Rahman's (1982) foundational critique of modern Islamism and its efforts to "Islamize" modern intellectual and social domains like politics, economics, education, and science. In considering American Islamic banking, however, and its potential impact on Islamic banking globally, I think these kinds of criticisms are beside the point. If Islamic banking historically was imagined by its promoters to lead eventually to the creation of an entirely separate economic system for the global umma (see, for example, Chapra 1985), Islamic banking in the United States *is defined by and becomes effective through its entanglements with conventional finance,* and this fact does not always undermine its "Islamic" character for those who participate in it. Instead, I have been arguing that those entanglements underwrite both the universal applicability of formal bureaucratic rationality *and* the universality of Islamic knowledge practices—and by extension, of Islam itself.

Those entanglements do sometimes cause concern and confusion among Muslim Americans who want to avoid riba and are not always certain whether or to what extent riba is the same as interest and how much they should worry about it. But these concerns also have spurred the creation of new mortgage markets, new market niches, and new client profiles. Mahmoud El-Gamal explained in an interview with the *Legal Times*:

> The name of the game is to try to maintain noticeable differences between conventional finance and Islamic finance in order to use the Islamic brand name, but then to convince regulators that it isn't so different. That's where interaction between Muslim jurists and lawyers comes in.[2]

A cynical reading of Islamic mortgage alternatives would hold that they are *only* about branding and market niche. For those involved in them and those who seek them out, however, they speak to broader issues about inclusion and participation in American civil society, as well as unfolding and ongoing debates over the nature and status of Islamic law. The "Islam" in Islamic mortgage may be simply an act of branding, but to paraphrase Clifford Geertz (1973), brands speak to epistemologies. And it is not just real estate but epistemologies—theories of knowledge and their potentially universal reach—that are at stake in Islamic home financing.

As they are in conventional mortgages. As explained in chapter 1, the conventional mortgage cannot be understood as a purely secular, rational affair. It is bound up in notions of intimate and ultimate order, questions of life and death, and the status of the eternal soul. The interplay between bureaucratic standardization and epistemological plurality is a characteristic not just of Islamic mortgages but of conventional ones as well. This has been the case from their very inception to their present place in structuring the patchwork of state laws, regulations, and interpretive work that governs them, and to their role in structuring the urban and suburban environments in which many of us live. Those environments are themselves simultaneously cause and effect of political decisions and philosophies of deep and lasting moral significance.

CHAPTER EIGHT

CONCLUSION

As we have seen, Islamic home financing at first proceeded in fits and starts. Several small local enterprises, cooperatives, and mosque-based organizations attempted various models of interest-free financing, but these efforts never achieved wider regional or national scope. Three events changed all this: the OCC interpretive rulings that declared lease-to-purchase and cost-plus arrangements a simple extension of a bank's mortgaging powers; the support given to Islamic home financing by Freddie Mac and other government-sponsored enterprises; and the impact of September 11, 2001, on Islamic banking and Muslim American identity. Another seminal event may have been the creation of sukuk—Islamic mortgage-backed securities for sale in international capital markets, although it is too early to tell.

As discussed in chapter 2, the OCC interpretive rulings mirrored the process of interpretation in Islamic law. A hallmark of modern, bureaucratic rationality is its supposedly infinite extendibility. Purely formal, it should be able to capture and contain any content. Its ability to do so tautologically underwrites its universality. If the OCC can accommodate all contingencies within its interpretive mandate, then that agency remains a truly impartial adjudicator that can rule from a position above the fray of the day-to-day transactions and debates of modern banking and finance. Islamic law's infinite extendibility derives from its connections to sacred sources and the word of God. Through its practices of interpretation, it demonstrates its own transcendence. A guide for humans through the travails and conflicts of life, it directs them down the godly, pious path. The different tributaries that make it up all flow into a great, universal river bringing humans closer and closer to God.

From the point of view of shari'a, the key feature of the OCC ruling is its interpretive nature. It is ijtihad. Indeed, it made use of a respected Islamic jurisprudential technique—reasoning by analogy, or qiyas—to arrive at the conclusion that ijara is simply another form of financing and not, strictly speaking, leasing, because the way it is used is functionally equivalent to a mortgage. Murabaha, similarly, is simply an extension of a bank's lending powers. Ijtihad and the interpretive rulings of the OCC thus reinforce one another, or to put it even more strongly, they mutually constitute one another in the process of their collaborative interpretive activity because each needs the other to warrant its claim to universality. That these two universally extendible, knowledge-generating forms flow together belies any simple statement that one is secular and the other religious. Instead, the secular and the religious are inextricably intertwined, and the category "modern" may name that condition of entanglement rather than stand on one side of the supposed opposition between secular and sacred (Latour 1993).

The involvement of government-sponsored enterprises like Fannie Mae and Freddie Mac has meant, above all, guaranteed and steady financing for Islamic home mortgages as well as standardized application forms and procedures. Standardization has helped professionalize the field. Clients of Islamic mortgage companies told me how much they appreciate filling out legal-looking forms when they apply for financing. They implied that other Muslim businesses act on trust or faith if their client is also Muslim, and they expressed suspicion of such a practice. The standardized form gives them the confidence that the company is legitimate from both an American law and a shari'a perspective. It also assures them that they are being given equal service. Standardized application forms have created an effect of anonymity that has had a positive value in the post-9/11 climate for Muslims who want to be treated just like everyone else.

The involvement of Freddie Mac and the use of standardized forms have also permitted Islamic home financing to occur on a whole new scale, geographically and metaphorically. Islamic home financing companies have now gone national. Ann Burkhart (2002) notes that mortgage law remains one of the least rationalized of any legal domain. In the wider field of conventional home finance, the participation of government-sponsored enterprises like Freddie Mac and Fannie Mae has produced a slow and creeping state-by-state standardization. The adoption of Freddie Mac application forms by Islamic financing companies has eased their entry into new states, so that their operations are now nearly truly national. The interesting paradox here is that a standard form has facilitated the growth of a niche product. Again, the secular and religious are not so much separate poles as intertwined.

Metaphorically, standardization means that Islamic mortgages can achieve universality and that they can produce universality in their subjects—that is, in the people who purchase them. Standard application forms, as I suggested in chapter 5, are a kind of print media that creates an imagined community of horizontal social ties that, despite their anonymity, bind people together in a larger public. This is particularly important as Muslim Americans come to experience themselves as a collectivity that is less marked by ethnic, factional, or sectarian differences and more by their demand for full political inclusion and cultural citizenship. As one interviewee put it bluntly, "What 9/11's done, of course, is sharpen [Muslim Americans'] already sharp focus on who they are and what they are, and it brings them closer together." Needless to say, "there is more than one Muslim identity," as Leonard (2003, 51) argues and numerous scholars have demonstrated. But standardized mortgage financing has combined with the impact of September 11 to produce at least the conditions of possibility for a Muslim identity that, like the paperwork, is standardized too—at least in some contexts and for some purposes. Meanwhile, the financial impact of September 11 also depressed the Islamic mutual fund and investment markets, and historically low interest rates put home financing on the front burner of every homeowner and potential homeowner in the United States.

The issuance of Islamic mortgage-backed securities extends the geographic and metaphorical potential of Islamic mortgages even further as a tool for universality. It re-creates what Freddie Mac has achieved within the United States, but at another level of scale. Global investors have been brought into the picture, and as Guidance's promotional material makes clear, that has happened within the same shari'a-compliant framework of the initial co-ownership mortgage. Just as Guidance is a co-owner with a home buyer and Freddie Mac is a co-owner with Guidance, international investors can now be co-owners with Freddie Mac, sharing the risk, spreading the profit, and, in the vision of some American Islamic bankers, spreading peace, justice, and the American way of business.

Furthermore, as discussed in previous chapters, Islamic mortgages may be animated by a form of routinized charisma, but not necessarily in the Weberian sense. In making a fatwa look like an American legal document and concretizing it on paper, and in mobilizing Freddie Mac mortgage application packets for mortgage seekers and for international investors, Islamic home financing is routinizing people's preexisting understanding of "law"—not what it does or what it is, but what it looks like, how it appears on paper. Prominent shaykhs can now derive their authority and achieve greater prominence by publicly signing such pieces of paper. This is not the charisma of office so much as the charisma of form.

And contra Weber, there is no clear evolutionary progression here from tradition to charisma to rational-legal authority. We have merely to consider the history told by Wael Hallaq (2001), discussed in chapter 5, of the ninth- and tenth-century shift from the age of ijtihad to the age of taqlid. Far from killing off juristic interpretation and rich and nuanced forms of legal reasoning, taqlid underwrote and gave life to renewed juristic creativity and plurality, together with and in spite of its purported aim to solidify doctrine and create determinacy in matters of fiqh. No, there is not here the kind of evolutionary progression that Weber foretold. Instead, there is a hybridization in which the supposedly "pure" original contributors to the new hybrid entail each other from the start. You cannot have Freddie Mac universalism without the particulars for it to work on, and you cannot have ijtihad without the OCC for it to work on. The standards, then, are already plural within themselves. Freddie Mac and sukuk, OCC rulings and ijtihad—each requires the other as its substantive warrant.

The intertwinings and hybrids of Islamic mortgages bring us back to the question of the ultimate translatability of riba and, indeed, of the Qur'an itself. Islamic banking, I have suggested, is not simply a collection of diverse and sometimes contradictory efforts to avoid riba, but the debate over riba itself, instantiated not only in discussions and arguments but in contractual forms and transactions. The objects of Islamic banking—the contracts, in other words—are already a part of their own analysis and critique. Similarly, during my research the distance between the object of study and the analysis of it collapsed as "interviews" turned into working discussions focused on trying to figure out—and to sketch, conjure, and adjudicate—the contractual forms of Islamic finance.

Social scientific dreams of a perfect language with which we might adequately capture all of social life, with which, ultimately, we might write the social into existence, always falter because they assume that words can be found that are adequate to things—that words re-present. Translation, in this misguided endeavor, is the search for a word that has a power analogous to the First Word in the monotheistic religions' conception of the making of the universe, a final word that can re-present wholly and without remainder. There is the presumption that translation brings us closer and closer to that original word, and thus to the world. Yet translation does not consist in the discovery of an original, for the original does not exist. Rather, translation, like all language, is iteration—the repetition and deferral of ultimate meaning, an endless striving toward . . . something. That something could be called Islam. It could equally be called America. It could also be called justice, or ethics. For the impossibility of translation is simultaneously the duty to make the attempt.

NOTES

GLOSSARY OF ARABIC TERMS

1. I have followed emerging international orthographic standards for these terms.

INTRODUCTION

1. As of April 30, 2005. See Dow Jones Islamic Market Index Statistics, available at: http://www.djindexes.com/mdsidx/index.cfm?event=showIslamicStats#cmc.
2. These figures include only loans for primary residences, not loans for multi-unit apartment buildings or business properties.
3. As discussed later, some Islamic mortgage products appear to constitute two transactions instead of one—a rental agreement plus a subsequent purchase. Stamp duties were levied on each of these transactions, effectively double-taxing Islamic mortgages in the United Kingdom.
4. Missouri Department of Insurance, "Credit History and Insurance FAQ," available at: http://www.insurance.state.mo.us/consumer/faq/creditScoring.htm.
5. Members of the U.S. Islamic banking community have privately prepared several proprietary studies.
6. Homeownership has long been the defining standard of the American dream; see Rohe and Stegman (1994), Rohe and Stewart (1995), and Wright (1981).
7. The work of law and society scholars has demonstrated the importance of understanding people's everyday legal consciousness—their folk understanding of what the law is and how it works—in explaining the relationships between law, society, identity, and citizenship; see, for example, Greenhouse (1986), Merry (1990), Yngvesson (1993).

CHAPTER 1

1. Marcel Mauss (1950, 48) discusses such pledges in his account of Roman and Germanic law. Mauss notes the connection of the Germanic wadium to the idea of a wager: "It is the prize of a competition and the sanction of a challenge even more directly than it is a means of constraint upon the debtor" (61). But there is danger in the pledge for the giver too, for he is bound to it just as much as the debtor. For Mauss, the pledge or wager demonstrates the peril and magic of the gift.
2. In title-theory states, the mortgagee's right of immediate possession is only theoretical prior to the borrower's default and the foreclosure of the mortgage. I am grateful to an anonymous reviewer for clarifying this point.
3. See American Finance House—LARIBA, "Lariba Concepts," available at: http://www.americanfinance.com/concepts.shtm.
4. All quotations from the Qur'an are taken from *The Koran: With Parallel Arabic Text*, translated by N. J. Dawood (London: Penguin Books, 2000).

CHAPTER 2

1. See, for example, John Daniszewski and Paul Watson, "Age-Old Way of Moving Cash Leaves Little Trail," *Los Angeles Times*, September 26, 2001. See DeGoede (2003) for a critique of the discourse on hawala and terrorist finance after 9/11.
2. See, for example, Susan Sachs, "Pursuing an American Dream While Following the Koran," *New York Times*, July 5, 2001.
3. "Introductory Remarks by John B. Taylor, Under Secretary for International Affairs, United States Treasury, at the Islamic Finance 101 Seminar Held at the U.S. Treasury Department, Washington, D.C.," April 26, 2002, PO-3068, Office of Public Affairs, available at: http://www.treas.gov/press/releases/po3068.htm.
4. Another important event after September 11, mentioned by almost all the industry professionals I interviewed, was the publication of a lengthy and sympathetic article on Islamic banking in *Fortune* magazine (Useem 2002).
5. These are the screens that guide the Dow Jones Islamic Market Indices and are generally recognized as the industry standard (see Dow Jones 1999).
6. The Timothy Plan funds screen out stocks of companies that offer same-sex domestic partner benefits, for example, while the Christian Science American Trust Allegiance Fund screens out medical stocks. The Carlisle Catholic indexes screen out companies that deal with contraception or pornography, but companies that have been charged with racial or gender discrimination or unfair lending practices, that trade with Myanmar/Burma, or that are involved with genetically modified organisms are screened out as well. Lumping these funds together with Islamic banking under the rubric of faith-

based investment options for religiously conservative individuals does not adequately capture the complexity here, as "conservatism" within one religious tradition is not commensurate with conservatism in another.

7. Islamic banking and finance employs Arabic terms from classical jurisprudence for its contractual forms. I set to one side here the interplay of Islamic jurisprudence and Arabic terms, on the one hand, and the dynamics of product positioning, on the other. See Maurer (2005) for a more complete discussion.

8. "Freddie Mac, Standard Federal Bank Announce New Islamic Home Financing Initiative for Michigan Families" (press release), August 10, 2001, available at: http://www.freddiemac.com/news/archives2001/sohinitiative0810.htm. See also "Freddie Mac Provides Lease-Purchase Mortgages for Muslims," *International Real Estate Digest*, September 4, 2001.

9. Edwin McDowell, "Financing Is Arranged for Observant Muslims," *New York Times*, February 14, 2003.

10. See "Islamic Home Financing Starting the Nation's Capital," *The Minaret* (July–August 2002): 19–20.

11. See Karen Dybis, "Banks Offer No-Interest Options for Muslims." *Detroit News*, December 21, 2004.

12. See Susan Sachs, "Pursuing an American Dream While Following the Koran," *New York Times*, July 5, 2001.

13. Freddie Mac's involvement with Islamic home finance came under the rubric of its "Summer of Homeownership" initiative, which sought to increase access for underserved populations, particularly lower-income individuals and immigrants.

14. Abdulkader Steven Thomas, the former general manager of UBK in New York who shepherded UBK's ijara and murabaha contracts through the OCC process, went on to help found Guidance Financial and to develop the SHAPE program. He is a prominent figure in the field of American Islamic mortgage alternatives and the author of the book *What Is Permissible Now?* (1995) and co-author of *The Guide to Understanding Islamic Home Finance* (Morris and Thomas 2002).

15. This fatwa is reproduced at http://www.islamonline.net/fatwa and in more complete form at http://www.dawoodi-bohras.com/chronicle.mar01.fatwa .htm.

16. The spiritual leader of the Muslim Brotherhood, al-Qaradawi is a controversial figure. One might assume from this discussion that his "permissive" views of interest make him controversial, and indeed, Saudi Wahhabis condemn his permissive views on artistic expression. He condemned the attacks of September 11 but has also been seen as a radical militant who advocates violence; he has been banned from traveling to the United States since 1999, and there were calls for him to be expelled from the United Kingdom in 2004 for alleged ties to terrorist financing. A rumor that he owned shares of

the Minneapolis-based Caribou Coffee Company caused that company's profits to plummet by 40 percent between 2002 and 2004. See Andrew Schroedtner, "Perpetual Email Kills North Shore Caribou Coffees," *Chicago Sun Times,* October 28, 2004; see also Alison Rowat, "Islamic Moderate or Public Rabble-Rouser?" *Glasgow Herald,* July 8, 2004.

17. Quoted in "Islamic Finances," *Religion and Ethics Newsweekly* (February 8), transcript available at: http://www.pbs.org/wnet/religionandethics/week523/p-feature.html.

18. "Hiyal (Legal Stratagems) and IBF," posted to ibfnet@yahoogroups.com, May 18, 2004.

19. Justice M. Taqi Usmani was a judge on the Shari'a Appellate Bench of the Supreme Court of Pakistan and is deputy chairman of the Islamic Fiqh Academy of the Organization of the Islamic Conference. He is also chairman of the shari'a supervisory board of the Guidance Financial Group. Besides serving on Guidance's shari'a supervisory board, Usmani has issued a fatwa or juristic ruling in favor of its Declining Balance Co-Ownership Program.

20. "Re: [IBF NET] Digest Number 944," posted to ibfnet@yahoogroups.com, December 30, 2004.

CHAPTER 3

1. Quoted and translated in Muhammad Akram Khan, *The Economic Teachings of the Prophet Muhammad* (Delhi: Noor Publishing House, 1992), 153–54; some punctuation removed to modernize the text.

CHAPTER 4

1. It is not clear whether these low denial rates mean that Muslim applicants are a better risk or that these mortgage providers have been able to prescreen their applicant pools.

2. Searchlight operates in California, Florida, Illinois, Maryland, Michigan, Minnesota, New Jersey, New York, Ohio, Pennsylvania, Virginia, and Washington, D.C. (as of 2005).

3. When more data become available, it will be interesting to see whether there are any effects of the different applicant pools on the profit margins of Islamic mortgage companies. This may be a task for the economists. Thanks to Karen Ahmed for posing the question.

4. $p < .000$; $\varphi = 0.4$ suggests a good relationship, while symmetric $\lambda = 0.21$ and λ with "lender" as dependent variable = 0.25 suggest a weak relationship.

5. $p < .000$; $\varphi = 0.24$; symmetric $\lambda = 0.317$; λ with "lender" as dependent variable = 0.317.

6. Kendall's $\tau - b = -0.12$; Kendall's $\tau - c = -0.14$; $\gamma = -0.2$.

7. I would like to thank Mike Burton for introducing me to loglinear analysis and recommending this analytical procedure for the data I am examining.

CHAPTER 6

1. U.S. Securities and Exchange Commission, "Mortgage-Backed Securities," available at: http://www.sec.gov/answers/mortgagesecurities.htm.
2. Such an increase through deferment is thus technically riba al-nasi'a, not riba al-fadl, or riba by excess. See Saleh (1986) for an extensive discussion of the distinctions between riba al-nasi'a and riba al-fadl and various juristic opinions on them. Historically, riba al-nasi'a has generally been forbidden more unambiguously than riba al-fadl.

CHAPTER 7

1. Still others argue that riba and interest are not equivalent terms and the edifice of Islamic banking is built on a self-interested mistranslation.
2. Lily Henning, "Dealing with Islam," *Legal Times*, May 29, 2003, available at: http://www.law.com/jsp/article.jsp?id=1052440798858. I would like to thank Gregory Starrett for bringing this article to my attention.

REFERENCES

Abdi Dualeh, Suleiman. 1998. "Islamic Securitisation: Practical Aspects." Paper presented to the World Conference on Islamic Banking. Geneva, Switzerland (July 8-9). Available at: http://www.guidancefinancialgroup.com/learn/ whitepapers.asp (accessed September 2, 2005).

Abdul-Rahman, Yahia, and Mike Abdelaaty. 2000. "The Capitalization of Islamic (Lariba) Finance Institutions in America." Paper presented to the Fourth International Harvard Islamic Finance Information Program Conference. Cambridge, Mass. (September 30).

Abdul-Rahman, Yahia, and Abdullah Tug. 1999. "Towards Lariba (Islamic) Mortgage Financing in the U.S.: Providing an Alternative to Traditional Mortgages." *International Journal of Islamic Financial Services* 1(2, July–September).

Abolafia, Mitchel Y. 1996. *Making Markets: Opportunism and Restraint on Wall Street*. Cambridge, Mass.: Harvard University Press.

Abou El Fadl, Khaled. 1998. "Striking a Balance: Islamic Legal Discourse on Muslim Minorities." In *Muslims on the Americanization Path?*, edited by Yvonne Haddad and John Esposito. Atlanta: Scholars Press.

Agresti, Alan. 1996. *An Introduction to Categorical Data Analysis*. New York: Wiley.

Al-Haddad, Haitham. 2004. "The Ruling on the Permissibility of Financing Properties Using Islamic Ijara Mortgages as Currently Implemented by HSBC and Other Banks" (December 12). Unpublished paper. Copy in author's possession.

AME Info.com. 2004. "Guidance Launches Innovative Islamic Securities Program to Mideast" (March 9). Available at: http://www.ameinfo.com/news/ Detailed/35934.html.

Anderson, Benedict. 1983. *Imagined Communities: Reflections on the Origin and Spread of Nationalism*. London: Verso.

Bagby, Ihsan, Paul Perl, and Bryan Froehle. 2001. *The Mosque in America: A Na-*

tional Portrait. Report from the Mosque Study Project. Washington, D.C.: Council on American-Islamic Relations.

Bank of England. 2003. "The Governor's Speech at the Islamic Home Finance Seminar on 27 March 2003." *Bank of England Quarterly Bulletin* 43(2): 240.

Beck, Thorsten, and Ian Webb. 2003. "Economic, Demographic, and Institutional Determinants of Life Insurance Consumption Across Countries." *World Bank Economic Review* 17(1): 51–88.

Bennett, Nicole, and Nikki Foster, with Margaret Tyndall. 2002. Alternative Financing: Issues and Opportunities for Lenders and Interest-Averse Populations. *Community Dividend* 1. Available at: http://minneapolisfed.org/pubs/cd/02-1/ (accessed September 2, 2005).

Burkhart, Ann M. 1999. "Lenders and Land." *Missouri Law Review* 64: 249–315.

———. 2002. "Mortgage." In *The Oxford Companion to American Law,* edited by Kermit L. Hall, David S. Clark, James W. Ely Jr., Joel Grossman, and N. E. H. Hull. Oxford: Oxford University Press.

Callon, Michel. 1998. "Introduction: The Embeddedness of Economic Markets in Economics." In *The Laws of the Markets,* edited by Michel Callon. Oxford: Blackwell.

Chakrabarty, Dipesh. 1989. *Rethinking Working-Class History: Bengal, 1840–1940.* Princeton, N.J.: Princeton University Press.

Chapra, M. Umer. 1985. *Towards a Just Monetary System.* Leicester, Eng.: Islamic Foundation.

Cole, Margaret, and Mohammed al-Sheikh. 2004. "The Growth of Sukuk in the Global Capital Markets." *AsiaLaw* (February 2). Available at: http://www.whitecase.com/publications/pubs_detail.aspx?pubid=2376&type=Articles (accessed September 2, 2005).

Day, Phillip, and S. Jayasankaran. 2003. "Deals and Deal Makers: Learning Islamic Finance—Banks Consult Muslim Experts in Bid to Tap Growing Market." *Wall Street Journal,* March 12.

DeGoede, Marieke. 2003. "Hawala Discourses and the War on Terrorist Finance." *Environment and Planning D: Society and Space* 21(5): 513–32.

DeLorenzo, Yusuf Talal. 1998. "The Fiqh Councilor in North America." In *Muslims on the Americanization Path?,* edited by Yvonne Haddad and John Esposito. Atlanta: Scholars Press.

Dow Jones. 1999. *The Dow Jones Islamic Market Index.* Booklet. New York: Dow Jones Company.

Dugaw, Dianne. 1998. "High Change in 'Change Alley': Popular Ballads and Emergent Capitalism in the Eighteenth Century." *Eighteenth-Century Life* 22(2): 43–58.

Ebrahim, Muhammed Shahid, and Zafar Hasan. 1993. "Mortgage Financing for Muslim-Americans." *American Journal of Islamic Social Sciences* 10(1): 72–87.

Eickelman, Dale, and Jon Anderson, eds. 1999. *New Media in the Muslim World: The Emerging Public Sphere.* Bloomington: Indiana University Press.

El-Gamal, Mahmoud. 1999. "An Economic Explication of the Prohibition of Riba in Classical Islamic Jurisprudence." Proceedings of the Third Harvard University Forum on Islamic Finance. Cambridge, Mass. (October 1).

———. 2000a. "An Introduction to Modern Islamic Economics and Finance." Proceedings of the Fourth Harvard University Forum on Islamic Finance. Cambridge, Mass. (September 30–October 1).

———. 2000b. "The Economics of Twenty-first-Century Islamic Jurisprudence." Proceedings of the Fourth Harvard University Forum on Islamic Finance. Cambridge, Mass. (September 30–October 1).

Fannie Mae Foundation. 2001. *Reaching the Immigrant Market: Creating Homeownership Opportunities for New Americans.* Washington: Fannie Mae Foundation.

Friendly, Michael. 2000. *Visualizing Categorical Data.* Cary, N.C.: SAS Institute.

Geertz, Clifford. 1973. *The Interpretation of Cultures.* New York: Basic Books.

Glanvill. 1998. *The Treatise on the Laws and Customs of the Realm of England Commonly Called Glanvill,* edited by G. D. G. Hall. Oxford: Clarendon Press.

Granovetter, Marc. 1985. "Economic Action and Social Structure: The Problem of Embeddedness." *American Journal of Sociology* 91: 481–510.

Greenhouse, Carol. 1986. *Praying for Justice: Faith, Order, and Community in an American Town.* Ithaca, N.Y.: Cornell University Press.

Guidance Financial. 2004. "The Declining Balance Co-ownership Program: An Overview." Available at: http://www.guidancefinancialgroup.com/learn/whitepapers.asp.

Haddad, Yvonne Yazbeck, and John L. Esposito, eds. 1998. *Muslims on the Americanization Path?* Oxford: Oxford University Press.

Hallaq, Wael. 2001. *Authority, Continuity and Change in Islamic Law.* Cambridge: Cambridge University Press.

Helleiner, Eric. 1994. *States and the Reemergence of Global Finance: From Bretton Woods to the 1990s.* Ithaca, N.Y.: Cornell University Press.

Hertz, Ellen. 1998. *The Trading Crowd: An Ethnography of the Shanghai Stock Market.* Cambridge: Cambridge University Press.

Holden, Arthur C. 1966. "The Interest Rate, Mortgage Debt, and Rent." *Land Economics* 41(2): 103–7.

Holdsworth, William. 1925. *A History of English Law.* London: Methuen.

Huck, Paul. 2001. "Home Mortgage Lending by Applicant Race: Do HMDA Figures Provide a Distorted Picture?" *Housing Policy Debate* 12(4): 719-36.

Ingrassia, Catherine. 1998. *Authorship, Commerce, and Gender in Early Eighteenth-Century England: A Culture of Paper Credit.* Cambridge: Cambridge University Press.

Jackson, Kenneth. 1987. *Crabgrass Frontier: The Suburbanization of the United States.* Oxford: Oxford University Press.

Janahi, Esam. 2004. "Continuing Innovation Must Characterize the Future of Islamic Finance." *Euromoney* 35(422, June): 8–10.

Kiyosaki, Robert T. and Sharon L. Lechter. 2000. *Rich Dad, Poor Dad: What The*

Rich Teach Their Kids About Money That The Poor and Middle Class Do Not.
New York: Warner Books.

Knorr Cetina, Karin, and Urs Bruegger. 2000. "The Market as an Object of Attachment: Exploring Postsocial Relations in Financial Markets." *Canadian Journal of Sociology* 25: 141–68.

Knorr Cetina, Karin, and Alex Preda. 2005. "Introduction." In *The Sociology of Financial Markets*, edited by Karin Knorr Cetina and Alex Preda. Oxford: Oxford University Press.

Kubis-Labiak, Barbara. 2004. *The U.K. Mortgages Market Outlook: Increasing Market Share Through Growing Niche Markets.* London: Business Insights.

Kuran, Timur. 2004. *Islam and Mammon: The Economic Predicaments of Islamism.* Princeton, N.J.: Princeton University Press.

Latour, Bruno. 1993. *We Have Never Been Modern.* Cambridge, Mass.: Harvard University Press.

Leonard, Karen Isaksen. 2003. *Muslims in the United States: The State of the Research.* New York: Russell Sage Foundation.

Listokin, David, Elvin Wyly, Brian Schmitt, and Ioan Voicu. 2001. "The Potential and Limitations of Mortgage Innovation in Fostering Homeownership in the United States." *Housing Policy Debate* 12(3): 465–513.

MacKenzie, Donald. 2003. "Long-Term Capital Management and the Sociology of Arbitrage." *Economy and Society* 32: 349–80.

Marshall, Alex. 2000. *How Cities Work: Suburbs, Sprawl, and the Roads Not Taken.* Austin: University of Texas Press.

Maurer, Bill. 1999. "Forget Locke? From Proprietor to Risk-Bearer in New Logics of Finance." *Public Culture* 11: 365–85.

———. 2005. *Mutual Life, Limited: Islamic Banking, Alternative Currencies, Lateral Reason.* Princeton, N.J.: Princeton University Press.

Mauss, Marcel. 1950. *The Gift: The Form and Reason for Exchange in Archaic Societies*, translated by Wilfred Douglas Halls. New York: W. W. Norton.

Merry, Sally Engel. 1990. *Getting Justice and Getting Even: Legal Consciousness Among Working-Class Americans.* Chicago: University of Chicago Press.

Minnesota Housing Finance Authority. 2002. *State of Minnesota Analysis of Impediments to Fair Housing, Federal Fiscal Year 2002.* Minneapolis: Minnesota Housing Finance Authority, Minnesota Department of Trade and Economic Development, and Minnesota Department of Children, Families, and Learning.

Miyazaki, Hirokazu. 2003. "The Temporalities of the Market." *American Anthropologist* 105: 255–65.

Moore, Kathleen. 1995. *Al-Mughtaribun: American Law and the Transformation of Muslim Life in the United States.* Albany: State University of New York Press.

Morris, Virginia B., and Abdulkader S. Thomas. 2002. *Guide to Understanding Islamic Home Finance in Accordance with Islamic Shari'ah.* New York: Lightbulb Press.

Munnell, Alicia H., Geoffrey Tootell, Lynne Browne, and James McEneaney. 1996. "Mortgage Lending in Boston: Interpreting HMDA Data." *American Economic Review* 86(1): 25–53.

Nelson, Benjamin. 1969. *The Idea of Usury: From Tribal Brotherhood to Universal Otherhood.* Chicago: University of Chicago Press.

New Jersey Citizen Action. 1997. *Women's Access to Mortgage Lending in New Jersey.* Policy report. Camden, N.J.: Rutgers University.

Office of the Comptroller of the Currency. 1997. Interpretive Letter #806. December. 12 U.S.C. 24(7); 12 U.S.C. 371.

———. 1999. Interpretive Letter #867. November 1999. 12 U.S.C. 24(7); 12 U.S.C. 29.

Osborne, George E. 1951/1970. *Handbook on the Law of Mortgages,* 2nd ed. St. Paul: West Publishing Co.

Papademetriou, Demetrios, and Brian Ray. 2004. "From Homeland to a Home: Immigrants and Homeownership in Urban America." *Fannie Mae Papers* 3(1): 1–16.

Pollack, Frederick, and Frederic William Maitland. 1909. *The History of English Law Before the Time of Edward I,* 2 vols. Cambridge: Cambridge University Press.

Pope, Hugh. 2005. "Islamic Banking Grows, with All Sorts of Rules." *Wall Street Journal,* May 3.

Pryke, Michael, and John Allen 2000. "Monetized Time-Space: Derivatives— Money's 'New Imaginary'?" *Economy and Society* 29: 264–84.

Rahman, Fazlur. 1982. *Islam and Modernity.* Chicago: University of Chicago Press.

Riles, Annelise. 1998. "Infinity Within the Brackets." *American Ethnologist* 25(3): 378–98.

———. 2004. "Real Time: Unwinding Technocratic and Anthropological Knowledge." *American Ethnologist* 31(3): 392–405.

Rohe, William, and Michael Stegman. 1994. "The Impact of Homeownership on the Social and Political Involvement of Low-Income People." *Urban Affairs Quarterly* 30(1): 28–50.

Rohe, William, and Leslie S. Stewart. 1995. "Homeownership and Neighborhood Stability." *Housing Policy Debate* 7(1): 37–82.

Ross, Stephen and John Yinger. 2002. *The Color of Credit: Mortgage Discrimination, Research Methodology, and Fair Lending Enforcement.* Cambridge, Mass.: MIT Press.

Saeed, Abdullah. 1998. "Idealism and Pragmatism in Islamic Banking: The Application of Shari'ah Principles and Adjustments." *Journal of Arabic, Islamic, and Middle Eastern Studies* 4(2): 89–111.

———. 1999. *Islamic Banking and Interest: A Study of the Prohibition of Riba and Its Contemporary Interpretation.* Leiden: E. J. Brill.

Said, Edward. 1978. *Orientalism.* New York: Pantheon.

Saleh, Nabil A. 1986. *Unlawful Gain and Legitimate Profit in Islamic Law.* Cambridge: Cambridge University Press.

Shell, Marc. 1982. *Money, Language, and Thought.* Berkeley: University of California Press.

————. 1995. *Art and Money.* Chicago: University of Chicago Press.

Simmel, Georg. 1907/1990. *The Philosophy of Money,* 2nd ed., edited by David Frisby. London: Routledge, 1990.

Squires, Gregory D., and Sally O'Connor. 2001. *Color and Money: Politics and Prospects for Community Reinvestment in Urban America.* Albany, N.Y.: State University of New York Press.

Stark, David. 2002. "The Economic Sociology of Value." Paper presented at the conference, "Empire of Economics." New York University (May 22–24).

Strathern, Marilyn. 1999. *Property, Substance, and Effect: Anthropological Essays on Persons and Things.* London: Althone Press.

————. 2004. *Commons and Borderlands. Working Papers on Interdisciplinarity, Accountability, and the Flow of Knowledge.* Oxon: Sean Kingston Publishing.

Thomas, Abdulkader Steven. 2001. "Methods of Islamic Home Finance in the United States: Beneficial Breakthroughs." Unpublished paper. Copy in author's possession.

————. 1995. *What Is Permissible Now!?* Singapore: Muslim Converts Association of Singapore and *American Journal of Islamic Finance.*

Thrift, Nigel. 2000. "Afterwords: Environment and Planning D." *Society and Space* 18: 213–55.

Tickell, Adam. 2000. "Dangerous Derivatives: Controlling and Creating Risks in International Money." *Geoforum* 31: 87–99.

Tsing, Anna. 2000. "Inside the Economy of Appearances." *Public Culture* 12: 115–44.

Tyndall, Margaret. 2001. "Islamic Finance and the U.S. Banking System." *Community Investments* 13(3): 17–19.

U.S. Department of Commerce. Bureau of the Census. 2005. *Statistical Abstract of the United States, 2004-2005.* Washington: U.S. Government Printing Office.

Useem, Jerry. 2002. "Banking on Allah." *Fortune* (June 10).

Vogel, Frank, and Samuel L. Hayes III. 1998. *Islamic Law and Finance: Religion, Risk, and Return.* The Hague: Kluwer Law International.

Warde, Ibrahim. 2000. *Islamic Finance in the Global Economy.* Edinburgh: Edinburgh University Press.

Watanabe, Teresa. 2001. "Private Studies Fuel Debate over Size of U.S. Muslim Population." *Los Angeles Times,* October 28.

Weber, Max. 1968. *Economy and Society: An Outline of Interpretive Sociology.* New York: Bedminster Press.

Wilson, Rodney, ed. 1990. *Islamic Financial Markets.* London: Routledge.

Wright, Gwendolyn. 1981. *Building the Dream: A Social History of Housing in America.* New York: Pantheon.

Wyly, Elvin, and Steve Holloway. 2002. "The Disappearance of Race in Mortgage Lending." *Economic Geography* 78(2): 129-69.

Yngvesson, Barbara. 1993. *Virtuous Citizens, Disruptive Subjects: Order and Complaint in a New England Court.* New York: Routledge.

Zaloom, Caitlin. 2003. "Ambiguous Numbers: Trading Technologies and Interpretation in Financial Markets." *American Ethnologist* 30: 258–72.

INDEX

Boldface numbers refer to figures and tables.

Abou El Fadl, K., 53, 54, 93
Accounting and Auditing Organization for Islamic Financial Institutions (AAOIFI), 30, 96
acculturation, 11
acquisition payments, 50
African Americans, 63
Ahli United Bank, 8
al-Haddad, H., 42
"alive" property, 48, **49**
al-Manzil, 34
al-Qaradawi, Y., 40, 49, 78, 105*n*16
Amana Growth Fund, 32
Ameen Housing Cooperative, 34
American Finance House—LARIBA, 24, 33, 34
Americanization, 6
American Jewish Committee, 8
American Religious Identification Survey, 8
amortization, 15–16
Anderson, B., 83
Anderson, J., 93
anonymity, 75, 83, 99
anthropology, 7–8
Aristotle, 17, 18, 19–20, 24
Ashley, W., 20

Bagby, I., 54
barter, 47
Bible, references to usury, 17–18
Bilal hadith, 45, 46, 50
Bradford, H., 42–43
branding, 1–2, 97
Burkhart, A., 20, 23, 82, 99
Burton, M., 107*n*7
Business Insights, 8

California, as community property state, 62
Callon, M., 5
capital, 19–20, 23
Caribou Coffee Company, 106*n*16
Carlisle Catholic indexes, 104*n*6
census data, 8
charismatic authority, 95–96, 101
Chicago, Islamic mortgages in, 35
Christians and Christianity, 18, 19–20, 33
Christian Science American Trust Allegiance Fund, 104*n*6
Citibank, 1
commercial mortgages, 22
common law, 2
Community Reinvestment Act (CRA) (1977), 22

conflicts of interest, 95
conservative Muslims, 53, 58, 73
contracts: ambiguity of, 42; Islamic
    security issuances, 87–88; istisna
    contracts, 87, 88; lease-to-own pro-
    grams or contracts, 35, 45, 47, 75,
    76–77; mudaraba contracts, 52, 75;
    musharaka contracts, 49–52; nego-
    tiable contracts, 87; research is-
    sues, 5. *See also* ijara contracts;
    murabaha contracts (cost-plus
    model)
conventional mortgages: HMDA
    data on, 57; vs. Islamic mortgages,
    37, 49; by lender, **61**; Muslims'
    use of, 40, 80; number vs. refinanc-
    ing applications, **15**; terms,
    36
conveyances, 18
co-ownership contracts, 49
corporate accountability and trans-
    parency, 30
corruption, 91
cost-plus model. *See* murabaha con-
    tracts (cost-plus model)
CRA (Community Reinvestment Act)
    (1977), 22
creditors. *See* lenders

Dallah al-Baraka, 34
darurah, 40
data sources, 42, 56–57, 76
"dead" property, 17, **49**
debt, 19, 20
DeLorenzo, Y., 24, 81
Devon Bank, 35
diminishing musharaka: vs. conven-
    tional mortgages, **37**; Ijara model,
    48; Muslims' understanding of, 75;
    terms, **36**
Domini Social Investments, 33
Dow Jones Islamic Market Index, 1
down payments, 65

economies, 5
Eickelman, D., 93
El-Gamal, M., 26–27, 41, 42, 47, 97
Emergency Home Finance Act
    (1970), 22
England, 4, 8, 17, 20, 42
environmental liability, 23–24
ethnography, 7, 76

fair lending monitoring and
    enforcement, 57
Faisal Finance Switzerland (FFS), 88
faith-based financial services, 32–33
Fannie Mae (Federal National Mort-
    gage Association), 3, 11, 22, 86
fatwas, 42, 49, 95
Federal Bureau of Investigation
    (FBI), 28
Federal Financial Institutions Exami-
    nation Council (FFIEC), 56
Federal Home Loan Mortgage Cor-
    poration (FHLMC or Freddie
    Mac): application forms, 82; com-
    mitment to underserved popula-
    tion, 3, 38; creation of, 22; invest-
    ment in Islamic mortgages, 34, 38;
    mortgaged-backed securities, 23,
    85, 86–87, 89, 90–91, 100; securiti-
    zation of Islamic mortgages,
    38–39; "Summer of Homeowner-
    ship" initiative, 105*n*13
Federal Housing Administration
    (FHA), 22
Federal Housing Enterprises Finan-
    cial Safety and Soundness Act
    (FHEFSSA), 11
Federal National Mortgage Association
    (FNMA or Fannie Mae), 3, 11, 22, 86
Federal Reserve Bank of Minneapolis,
    35
FFIEC (Federal Financial Institu-
    tions Examination Council), 56
FFS (Faisal Finance Switzerland), 88

FHA (Federal Housing Administration), 22
FHEFSSA (Federal Housing Enterprises Financial Safety and Soundness Act), 11
fieldwork, 4
finance and financial markets, 5
Financial Services Modernization Act (1999), 38
fiqh, 2, 93
Fiqh Council of North America, 54
Fortune magazine, 104*n*4
Freddie Mac. *See* Federal Home Loan Mortgage Corporation (FHLMC or Freddie Mac)
Froehle, B., 54

gages of land, 17
Geertz, C., 97
gender issues, 61–62, 65–73
Glanvill, 17
Government National Mortgage Association (GNMA or Ginnie Mae), 22, 86
Great Britain, 4, 8, 17, 20, 42
Guidance Financial Group, 24, 34, 42, 85, 87, 88, 90, 100
Guide to Understanding Islamic Home Finance in Accordance with Islamic Shari'ah, 24

Haddad, H. al-, 42
Hallaq, W., 84, 101
Harvard Islamic Finance Information program, 26
Hashim, H., 85
Hayes, S., 2
History of English Land Law Before the Time of Edward I (Pollack and Maitland), 16–17
Holden, A., 15–16
Home Mortgage Disclosure Act (HMDA) data, 56–57

homeownership: and acculturation, 11; as American dream standard, 103*n*6; incentives for, 14; and middle class identity, 6; and political evolution of Muslims, 38; and poverty, 10
HSBC, 8, 35, 42

IBFNet Internet listserv, 42–43, 94
IDB (Islamic Development Bank), 87
identity, 6
ijara contracts: companies offering, 34, 35; vs. conventional mortgages, **37**; Ijara's model, 44–49; Islamic security issuance, 88; lessee as titleholder, 47; vs. musharaka contracts, 50; scholars' debate over, 52; terms, **36**
Ijara (Islamic finance company): consumers drawn to, 53, 55, 73; vs. conventional mortgages, **49**; down payment requirements, 65; female vs. male applicants, **62, 65**; geographic distribution of lending activity, 59, **60**, 82; income of applicants, 63–65, **66**, 69–70; joint applications, 61, **62**; loan application process, 82–83; loan denial rates, 58; marketing tactics, 54; mortgage replacement model, 44–49; name recognition, 80; number of conventional loans vs. refinancing applications, 59, 61; odds of choosing over Searchlight, 65–73; perceived high cost of, 80–81; racial data, 63; vs. Searchlight, 78–84; shari'a compliance, 54–55, 81, 84
ijtihad: and debate over usury, 2; OCC ruling as, 39–40, 99; transition from, 84, 101; in U.S., 93
immigrants, 9, 26

income, 62, 63–73
Institute of Islamic Banking and
    Insurance, 26
interest, historical background of, 18,
    20. *See also* riba
interest deduction, 14–16, 48, 52
Internet listserv, IBFNet, 42–43, 94
Interpretive letters, 39, 40. *See also*
    ijtihad; Office of the Comptroller of
    the Currency (OCC)
interviews, 76
investment vehicles, 31–33, 86–92
Islam, in U.S. *See* Muslims, in U.S.
Islamic banking and finance: activities
    of, 25–26; after 9/11, 29–30; defi-
    nition of, 26; entanglements with
    conventional finance, 96; growth
    of, 1, 28; historical background, 26;
    and interpretive letters, 39, 40; in-
    vestment vehicles, 31–33, 86–92;
    Islamic terms for contractual
    forms, 26; theoretical considera-
    tions, 2. *See also* Islamic mortgages
Islamic charities, 28, 32
Islamic Circle of North America, 26,
    34, 53
Islamic Development Bank (IDB), 87
Islamic investment vehicles, 31–33,
    86–92
Islamic law. *See* shari'a
Islamic Market Index Growth Fund,
    32
Islamic mortgage alternative. *See*
    Islamic mortgages
Islamic mortgage replacement prod-
    ucts. *See* Islamic mortgages
Islamic mortgages: companies offer-
    ing, 2, 33–35; vs. conventional
    mortgages, 35; debates over, 27,
    41–43, 52–53; definition of, 4, 43;
    demographic characteristics of ap-
    plicants, 56; Freddie Mac's invest-
    ment in, 34, 38–39; growth of, 3,

11; loan application process, 82–83;
    marketing of, 97; Muslims' under-
    standing of, 75, 76–78; origins of,
    33–34; and securitization, 90–91;
    shari'a compliance, 75–76; in U.K.,
    8–9; waiting lists for, 35. *See also*
    Ijara (Islamic finance company);
    Searchlight
Islamic Society of North America, 26,
    53
istisna contracts, 87, 88

Jesus Christ, 18
Jews, 17
joint applications, 61–62, 65, 70–71

Kuran, T., 1, 96

land, pledged as living or dead, 19–20
leases, **36,** 39, 42, 87. *See also* ijara
    contracts
lease-to-own programs or contracts,
    35, 45, 47, 75, 76–77
legal consciousness, 103n7
Legal Times, 97
lenders: data from, 56–57; distancing
    from borrowers with secondary
    market, 21–24; environmental lia-
    bility, 23–24; risk assumed, 19, 25.
    See also Ijara (Islamic finance com-
    pany); Searchlight
Leonard, K., 53, 54, 63, 93, 100
liens, 47
lien-theory states, 21
life insurance, 9
limited liability companies, 49–50
listservs, IBFNet, 42–43, 94
Littleton's Tenures, 19
loan denial rates, 58
loglinear analysis, 66

Maitland, F., 16–17
Malinowski, B., 7

MALT (Mortgage Alternative Loan Transaction), 35, 41
marketing, 54, 57, 97
markup, 33, 41–42, 50, 52, 87
Mauss, M., 104*n*1
MBSs (mortgaged-backed securities), 86–92
media, 41
methodology, 4, 7, 66
Michigan, Islamic mortgages in, 35
Minnesota, Islamic mortgages in, 35
Missouri Department of Insurance, 9
money, "natural" use of, 18
mortgaged-backed securities (MBSs), 86–92
mortgage law: rationality of, 99; state variances in, 21
mortgages: conventional vs. refinancing applications, **15**; by gender and income, **69**; vs. halal home acquisition agreements, 24; historical background, 16–24; meaning of, 14–15; secondary market for, 21–23; securing process, 21; standardization, 23; usurious nature of, 17–19. *See also* conventional mortgages; Islamic mortgages
MSI, 34
mudaraba contracts, 52, 75
murabaha contracts (cost-plus model): companies offering, 33, 35; Islamic security issuances, 87, 88; Muslims' understanding of, 75; OCC's interpretation of, 39–40; scholars' debate over, 52; tax reporting of markup, 41; terms, **36**
musharaka contracts, 49–52. *See also* diminishing musharaka
Muslim Brotherhood, 105*n*16
Muslim Council of Britain, 8
Muslims, in U.S.: as immigrants, 9; conservative, 53, 58, 73; number of, 8; progressive, 53, 58, 73; research considerations, 5–6; as underserved population, 9–10
mutual funds, 31–33

National Bank Act, 38
negotiable contracts, 87
9/11/01, 5–6, 28–30, 32, 38
Northside Residents Redevelopment Council, 35

Office of the Comptroller of the Currency (OCC), 3, 34, 39–40, 41, 98–99
offshore accounts, 88
O'Neill, P., 30

partnerships, **36**, 45, 49, 50, 52
Perl, P., 54
Politics (Aristotle), 18
Pollack, F., 16–17
poverty, 10
professionalism, 75, 82
profit, 48, 50, 52, 80
progressive Muslims, 53, 58, 73
public good, 24

Qaradawi, Y. al-, 40, 49, 78, 105*n*16
Qur'an, 25, 54

racial issues, 10, 57, 62–63
Rahman, F., 96
Reba-Free, 35
redlining, 22
refinancing loans: HMDA data, 57; Islamic mortgages, 59, 61; by lender, **61**; number of applications, **15**
Religion and Ethics Newsweekly, 41
religious affiliation, 8
rent, 45, 48, 50, 87
renters, 14–15
rent-to-own programs or contracts, 35, 45, 47, 75, 76–77

research issues, 2–3, 5

riba: lack of consensus about, 79; prohibitions against, 25, 27, 41; translations of, 24, 26, 41, 101–2

risk, 19, 25

Saeed, A., 1–2, 75, 88

Saleh, N., 107*n*2

scalability, 39

scholars, 3, 78–79, 81–82, 83

scriptures, interpretation of. *See* ijtihad

Searchlight: consumers drawn to, 53, 55, 73; conventional vs. refinancing applications, 59, 61; down payments, 65; female vs. male applicants, **62, 65**; geographic distribution of lending activity, 59, **60**, 82, 106*n*2; vs. Ijara, 78–84; income of applicants, 63–65, **66,** 69–70; joint applications, **62**; loan application process, 82–83; loan denial rates, 58; marketing, 54, 57; model of, 49–52; name recognition, 80; odds of choosing over Ijara, 65–73; professionalism of, 75, 82; racial data, 63; shari'a advisors and endorsements, 49, 54, 55, 81–82, 83

secondary market, for mortgages, 21–23, 39, 50

securities, mortgaged-backed (MBSs), 86–92

Securities and Exchange Commission (SEC), 86

securitization: benefits of, 90–92; definition of, 21; and lenders' distance from property, 21, 89; Muslims' skepticism about, 88–90; origins of, 85–86, 88; process of, 86–87; and scalability, 39

security, house as, 21

September 11, 2001, 5–6, 28–30, 32, 38

SHAPE, 35, 41

shari'a: change in, 84; contracts, 88; and debate over usury, 2; Ijara vs. Searchlight's model, 52, 54–55, 73, 74, 80, 81, 83–84; and mortgaged-backed securities, 86; Muslims' understanding of, 75–76; plurality of, 94–95; scholarship on, 6; in U.S., 53–54, 95

Shell, M., 18

Shi'a Muslims, 63

Simmel, G., 23

social ties, 23

St. Paul Neighborhood Development Center, 35

Standard Federal Bank, 34

standardization, 23, 27, 82, 91–92, 99–100

stock market downturn (2002), 32

Strathern, M., 7–8

sukuk, 87, 88, 98

Sunnah, 54

Sunni Muslims, 63

taqlid, 84, 101

tax implications, 14–16, 41, 48, 49, 52

Taylor, J., 30, 104*n*3

terrorism, 28, 29

Thomas, A., 105*n*14

Timothy Plan, 33, 104*n*6

title, holding of, 47–48

title-theory states, 21, 104*n*2

trade, 18, 47

Treasury Department, 1, 28

underserved populations, 9–10, 38, 105*n*13

United Bank of Kuwait (UBK), 8, 34, 39, 105*n*14

United Kingdom, 4, 8, 17, 20, 42
United Mortgage of America, 34
United National Bank, 8
University Bank, 35
U.S. census, 8
Usmani, M., 42, 81, 106n19
usury, 2, 17–19, 20, 24, 25. *See also* riba

vif-gage, 16, 17, 19, 44, 48
Vogel, F., 2

wealth, mortgages as source of, 14
Weber, M., 95, 101
women, 58–59, 61–62

Zarka, M., 94